THE INFLUENCE OF MYSTICISM
ON THE THEOLOGY OF JOHN WESLEY

Ernest R. Rugenstein PhD

THE INFLUENCE OF MYSTICISM
ON THE THEOLOGY OF JOHN WESLEY

ZADKIEL PUBLISHING

ISBN: 978-1-78695-605-7

This Edition
Published 2021
Zadkiel Publishing is an imprint of
Fiction4All
www.fiction4all.com

Preface

The genesis of this book came from my master thesis of the same title for an MA in Ministry/Religion. I have since earned an MA in European History and PhD n Cultural History.

Interest in the topic came from the course work for the Ministry/Religion degree and being an ordained minister (at the time,13-years) and the significance of the denominational distinctives of the organization I was connected to in 1999.

I was ordained in the *Full Gospel Methodist Church* headquartered in Rochester, NY in 1986 (Licensed 1984) serving as an Evangelist. In 1988, while ministering as a youth leader in a local *Wesleyan Church* in Ogdensburg, NY, I began the process of transferring my ordination. During this time, I started filling pulpits finalizing my transfer in 1992 and entering pastoral ministry shortly thereafter. While an ordained minister in the *Wesleyan Church* I served as a pastor in three different churches, served as the Director of Christian Education and of District Youth in the Easter New York – New England District, retiring from ministry in 2006.

The Wesleyan Church came about from the unification of the *Wesleyan Methodist Church* and the *Pilgrim Holiness Church* in 1968. The *Wesleyan Methodist Church* (an abolitionist church) separated from the *Methodist Episcopal Church* in 1843. *The*

Methodist Episcopal Church had its beginnings in the Great Awakening of the 1730's & 1740's with Methodism (which originated with John Wesley) spreading across the colonies by the 1760's. John Wesley ordained the first ministers in 1784. In 1968 the *Methodist Episcopal Church* and the *Evangelical United Brethren* united to form the *United Methodist Church*.

Methodist denominations have Wesley's theology in common and the distinctive of not just justification by faith but additionally the distinctives of sanctification and entire sanctification, the idea of Christian perfection.

This concept of Christian perfection fascinated me; to be perfect, how? How did this theology of John Wesley come about? How is it actuated? Was mysticism involved? This is what led me to the thesis and later to this book.

Rev. Dr. Ernest R. Rugenstein

6

Contents

Figures

Introduction

When the majority of people hear the word "mystic" or "mysticism" a certain interpretation is enjoined, and certain images arise. Frequently when people hear or read the word mystic, they automatically assume Eastern Mysticism with its beliefs and practices. To others the New Age movement with its mysticism and somewhat cultish followers is proffered as an ideological possibility. Still there are those who think of Christian mystics, those who sat on poles, in trees, or lived in caves to prove their devotion to God and to experience a special closeness.

There is no doubt that mysticism has long been part of the Christian church. Certainly, we find it in the "Old" Testament as well as in the Gospels and Epistles. The best example of mysticism in the New Testament is the Day of Pentecost. This is Biblically specified as the presence of the "Holy Spirit" falling upon the crowd with "tongues of fire" upon their heads allowing them to speak in other languages. It was seen in a Biblical sense as a union between God and humanity with outright manifestations.

Christian mysticism didn't disappear at the close of the Apostolic Age nor was it resigned to the ascetics. Many within the church saw it as a viable expression of divine interaction changing the believer with subtle changes over a long period of time or in some cases catastrophic in the blink-of-an-eye change. An investigation into Christian mystics such as Saint Teresa, Francis de Sales, Gregory of Nyssa, Thomas á Kempis, William Law and others who show that they wrote or testified to this mystical experience having a dramatic impact on their lives.

What's interesting is that these mystical experiences not only affect the individual, but through the individual it can affect institutions, ideologies, and denominations around the world. Sometimes it affects the understanding of the Eucharist as to whether it take the form of transubstantiation, consubstantiation, or is it simply a memorial to what was taught in scriptures. Other times it seems to manifest itself in the process of salvation or even in forms of personal piety. Mysticism has been seen to manifest in all forms of Christianity. It has found expression from the cult-like such as the Shakers and the Oneida Community to those who are socially accepted as more fundamental Christian denominations, for example Pentecostal, Charismatic, Evangelical and Holiness movements, to mainline Protestant denominations and of course the Catholic church. The Holy Catholic Church and its present iteration the Roman Catholic Church has for centuries acknowledged and generally accepted the mystics within their midst. Even though some in the church may not have readily accepted these mystics they none the less realize the richness they added to the church.

When we look at the how mysticism was an influence, we find that the founders of these denominations or at least significant influencers had been either positively or negatively influenced by an experience that they labeled as mystical. When we look at these individuals who had such an impact we find people from Mother Ann Lee, John Noyes, Madam Guyon, Joseph Smith, Charles Fox Parham, to Saint Teresa , Francis de Sales, Gregory of Nyssa, Thomas á Kempis, Meister Eckhart, William Law. It is supposed by many that John Wesley who was one of the founders of Methodism was also affected by a mystical experience.

Bishop William R. Cannon, Bishop of the United Methodist Church, stated in the forward of Dr. Robert G. Tuttle's monograph, *Mysticism in the Wesleyan Tradition*, that Rev. John Wesley was highly influenced by Christian mysticism and that it formed the essences of his Doctrine of Christian Perfection.[1] However, there are those who feel Wesley wasn't just influenced but was a mystic himself.

Wesley both praised and condemned mysticism a number of times both before and after his Aldersgate experience. Wesley was in a group reading of Luther's introduction to the *Epistle to the Romans* and as they were reading Luther's description of the alteration God makes in man's

---

[1] Robert G, Tuttle, Jr. Mysticism in the Wesleyan Tradition (Grand Rapids Michigan: Francis Asbury Press, 1989), 14.

heart, he underwent a conversion experience. Luther said he had his assurance of salvation where his intellectual conviction was changed into a personal experience.[2]

The book is divided into six major sections. The first of which is entitled *Definitions and Terms*. Because the terms used in the book can have varied definitions and connotation the 'chapter' of the book gives a common understanding to each,

What is mysticism is covered in the first chapter. Various mystics and types of mysticism are investigated in this chapter and give us an introduction to *Chapter 2: The Mystics in john Wesley's Life*. It is here we see how widely read Wesley was on the subject even reading mystics he disagreed with.

One of the mystics Wesley was fascinated with from a young age was Thomas á Kempis. Kempis was a favorite of Wesley's mother, and she encouraged John Wesley to internalize his distinctives and writings. Chapter 3 investigates this intellectual interaction between Kempis and Wesley.

Chapter 4 takes a closer look at mysticism and the effect it had on Wesley's theology with

---

[2] Holidays, Festivals, and Celebrations of the World Dictionary, Fourth Edition. S.v. "Aldersgate Experience." Retrieved June 22, 2020 from https://encyclopedia2.thefreedictionary.com/Aldersgate+Experience

Kempis' mysticism at the base of it. The final section is a literature review of some of the more important sources used.

It is well known that Wesley was well read in the writings of the mystics and even praised a few, yet it seems many believe that Wesley's theology hadn't any connection to mysticism at all. So, the question some may ask: Did mysticism have an influence on John Wesley's theology?

Definitions and Terms

There are a number of terms and definitions that are used in the book that have various meanings in our society today. So that there is a common bases of comparison and understanding the following definitions and terns will be implied when these terms are used. Naturally, the first of these definitions is that of *Mysticism*. When the term is applied here it is understood to be divine or semi-divine forces and/or beings through experience rather than through logical reasoning or pure intellect. Mystics tend to go through a number of stages to reach their ultimate goal. These usually include a stage of purification, a stage of illumination, and finally a stage that includes a union with the one being sought. Between the stages if illumination and union there may also appear a time of darkness and disorientation, a time of searching and not finding. Many times, special rites or rituals are employed during this time.

Another definition that is similar but not the same as *Mysticism* is *Christian Mysticism*. The difference is basically semantics with the difference being that they aspire to connect to the "one-true" God, through His Holy Spirit. They desire to know God directly and intimately and it may include a divinely initiated experience they find void of intellectual knowledge or rationality. Christian mystics go through stages similar to their non-Christian counterparts and include a period of purification, a period of illumination, and a period of union with God. There is also a phenomenon that occurs between illumination and union and is usually referred to as the 'Dark Night of the Soul.' It's a time of soul searching, and blind faith and it is during this time the Christian Mystic would be focused on Theocentric or Christocentric contemplation. A way of contemplation of one's soul in the light of either God the Father or Christ the Son.

The results of this contemplation for the Christian mystic are speculative and practical in nature. It's the combination of the internal evidence and unshakable faith with the external life of constant service to God and humanity. The Christian mystic sees service as a call to entering suffering and patterning and motivating of emotions in such a way that the aspirant won't shun the Cross for the materialism of the world. The definition of *Christian Mysticism* excludes any form of legalism being employed as a means of attaining union with God.

Legalism in its most basic definition in the sense of the topic is salvation by works instead of by grace, however, it is also to be understood as a system of theology that accepts salvation by grace but codifies behavior by rigid rules of conduct and thought.[3]

Since the study deals with John Wesley a term he uses, Christian Perfection, should also be defined. We will use Wesley's definition of it found in his writings *A Plain Account of Christian Perfection*. Christian Perfection is purity of intention, dedicating all life to God. It is the circumcision of the heart of all filthiness, all inward as well as outward pollution, the loving of God with all our hearts and our neighbors as ourselves.[4]

Finally, some attention needs to be paid by the Wesleyan/Holiness distinctive of *Sanctification*. The concept comes out of the Wesleyan Methodist and Pilgrim Holiness denominations and was adopted by the Wesleyan Church when the two organizations combined. The theology of the distinctive is outlined in the Wesleyan Discipline under the heading *Sanctification: Initial, Progressive, Entire*. It states:

> We believe that sanctification is that work of the Holy Spirit by which the child of God is separated from sin unto God and is enabled to love God with all the heart and to walk in all His holy commandments blameless.

---

[3] Irving Hexman, *Concise Dictionary of Religion* (Downers Grove, Illinois: Intervarsity Press, 1993) 135.

[4] John Wesley, *A Plain Account of Christian Perfection* ([1777] ed. Thomas Jackson (1872)] ed. George Lyons, (Nampa, ID: Northwest Nazarene College, 1996)), 87.

Sanctification is initiated at the moment of justification and regeneration. From that moment there is a gradual or progressive sanctification as the believer walks with God and daily grows in grace and in a more perfect obedience to God. This prepares for the crisis of entire sanctification which is wrought instantaneously when believers present themselves as living sacrifices, holy and acceptable to God, through faith in Jesus Christ, being effected by the baptism with the Holy Spirit who cleanses the heart from all inbred sin. The crisis of entire sanctification perfects the believer in love and empowers that person for effective service. It is followed by lifelong growth in grace and the knowledge of our Lord and Savior, Jesus Christ. The life of holiness continues through faith in the sanctifying blood of Christ and evidences itself by loving obedience to God's revealed will.[5]

With the review of these definitions and terms it gives a base to the further investigation into Wesley and the impact mysticism had on him and the institutions that are based on his theology.

---

[5] Anita Eastlack, Kerry D. Kind, Jerry Lumston, Matthew Pickering, Mark A. Rennaker, Johanna Rugh, Ronald C. McClung, co-chair, and Janelle Vernon, chair, *The Discipline of the Wesleyan Church 2016*, (Indianapolis, Indiana: Wesleyan Publishing House, 2016) 21.

Chapter 1 - What is Mysticism?

Mysticism has been with us from the very beginning of history and has "its origin in that which is raw material of religion . . .namely that dim consciousness of the beyond which is part of the nature of all human beings."[6] The word *Mysticism* and to the lesser extent *Mystic* can be found in practically all literature of a religious nature and with various definitions. These definitions either "describe a motley gallery of vaguely spiritual or psychical experiences. . . [or they are] . . . linked in the popular imagination with the darker aspects of lunacies of western esoteric tradition."[7] Most religious world views have their mystical element and applied it to numerous forms of theosophy, animalism, spiritualism, and meditation. Islam has Sufis, the Hindus have their holy men and gurus, Buddhist have "enlighten ones" and most New Age expressions have their forms of mystical transcendentalism.

From a Christian perspective this sort of mysticism relies on the occult in one form or another. Occult mysticism can be classed in either some form of natural mysticism dealing with divination, second sight, or superstitions, or a form

---

[6] W.R. Inge, *Christian Mysticism* (London: Methuse, 1899) 5.
[7] Michael Cox, *Handbook of Christian Spirituality* (San Francisco: Harper & Row Publishers, 1983), 20.

of mysticism that includes possession, witchcraft, and other assorted stories of terror.[8]

Classical Christian scholars assert that our understanding of God comes in three revelations.[9] The first of these proclaimed revelations is the natural world. It is this revelation of God that comes through a tree, stars in the sky, or a baby's birth. Christians believe this could not just happen; there is a certain order and reason for occurrences of events. It is through this "natural theology" that Christians see the natural works of God.[10] The next revelation God used is history, The scholarly idea is that God is in all aspects of history in both the pagan and orthodox religious world. God is self-revealed in Biblical/Quran text to the Hebrews first and the Gentiles next through Christianity and later Islam. In Christian theology this includes the aspect that Jesus is the propitiation for sin. This could be classified as "dogmatic theology."[11] Finally, the revelation of God is found through the soul's secret and direct union with God. In Christianity this is through a Theocentric or Christocentric experience or expression through the cultivation of a holy inner life. A holy life starting with prayer and a

---

[8] Inge, *Christian Mysticism*, 265.
[9] Evelyn Underhill, *The Mystics of the Church* (New York: Schocken Books, 1964) 14, 15.
[10] *Ibid.*
[11] *Ibid.*

willingness to seek God is called "mystical theology" or "Christian Mysticism."[12]

Theocentric contemplation in mysticism sets the course for the mystic to ascend to from God's reflection in the things He has created to his divine attributes.[13] A discipline attentiveness to nature is a way to have a disciplined attentiveness to God. The painter of a landscape takes the natural world and through patient, attentive and unselfish regard, transforms the simple unreflecting gaze of the masses into the contemplation of a subject.[14] Theocentric mysticism looks at the visible universe, with all its beauty and symmetry and perfection of form, and sees it as a manifestation of God's mind.[15] As the mystic looks at the visible world they see the invisible. Numbered among the Theocentric Christian mystics is Saint Augustine who originated the premise that through simple contemplation of creation we draw closer to God.

Christocentric mystical contemplation as the title implies is the ascent to union with God through Christ.[16] The dominate emotion is intimate affection and emphasizes the personal and incarnational rather than the abstract and Trinitarian side of

---

[12] *Ibid.*
[13] Cox, *Handbook of Christian*, 36
[14] Evelyn Underhill, *Man and the Supernatural* (New York: E.P. Dutton & Co., Inc., 1931), 193.
[15] Cox, *Handbook of Christian*, 37.
[16] *Ibid.*, 35.

Christianity.[17] Christocentric contemplation is governed by love that casts out fear; God, grace, and Jesus all in one.[18] It is characterized by the predominating sense of nearness, intimacy, and sweetness, rather than strangeness and unattainable transcendence.[19] As the Christ, Jesus is more than the focal point of Christianity. To His disciples Jesus was not just a prophet, or a style of life, or some divine figure from the past, but to them He was a present tense experience that was a communion of the most vivid kind. This unbroken and ceaseless communion has been claimed by Christians as the true supply of the church's undying energy.[20]

"Christian mysticism has its roots in pre-Christian history."[21] When the voice of God spoke to Paul/Saul on the road to Damascus God address one who knew the truths of the "Old" Testament [OT] and one who recognized an experience with God. The knowledge came from Saul's/Paul's Pharisaic training concerning the "Spirit of God" coming upon the prophets. There was confidence that direct interaction with God was a reality and a quality of all the greatest OT writers and the Jewish

---

[17] Evelyn Underhill, *Mysticism: A Study in the Nature and Development of a Man's Spiritual Consciousness* (New York: E.P. Dutton & Co., Inc., 1961), 342.
[18] Underhill, *The Mystics of the Church.*, 24.
[19] Underhill, *Mysticism: A Study*, 342
[20] Underhill, *The Mystics of the Church.*, 24.
[21] *Ibid.*, 30.

religion as a whole.[22] Therefore, it was not an unbelievable event for a mythical connection to God amongst the early Jews. Saul's/Paul's "Damascus Road" experience, although a surprise, was not unbelievable and for into the mystical possibilities of the Jewish faith and culture at the time. There was no difficulty in the idea that the "Damascus Road" experience was something that mystical and divine.

The "Damascus Road" occurrence was not the first in the New Testament [NT]. The incarnation was the quintessential mystical experience, the literal union in a physical and spiritual sense of God and humanity. This is not the only NT example of a mystical union. Pentecost[23] is another example of a mass mystical experience with humanity under the control of the Holy Spirit. "It is evident that the disciples were Christians before Pentecost and that something happened at Pentecost that dramatically changed their inner spiritual response as well as their outer spiritual expression."[24] Within the Christian traditions it's found that when the heart is

---

[22] *Ibid.*

[23] Pentecost is the Christian festival celebrating the descent of the Holy Spirit on the disciples of Jesus after his Ascension, held on the seventh Sunday after Easter. It is also called *Feast of Weeks, Shavuot* Judaism the harvest festival celebrated fifty days after the second day of Passover on the sixth and seventh days of Sivan, and commemorating the giving the Torah on Mount Sinai

[24] Donald S. Metz, *Studies in Biblical Holiness* (Kansas City, Missouri: Beacon Hill Press, 1971) 115.

"purified" by the Holy Spirit there is a change in the person from being fearful, unstable, and alone spiritually to someone who is being bold, courageous and with a oneness of heart.[25] Paul's/Saul's mystical experience was a participation between him and the Second Person of the Godhood.

The majority of the NT is a collection of letters written by a mystic. That is not to say that Paul/Saul was the only mystical writer or the only one with mystical experiences, however, he was the most prolific writer in the NT. His mystical writing can be seen in "the Epistle to the Galatians [where] he uses the favorite mystical phrase 'until Christ is formed in you' and in the Second Epistle to the Corinthians [where] he employs a most beautiful expression in describing the process, reverting to the figure of the 'mirror,' dear to Mysticism which he already used in the First Epistle."[26] Certainly in Second Corinthians 12:2 we find a mystical experience described where Paul/Saul writes of being caught up to the 'Third Heaven' with only God knowing if it was in the flesh or in the spirit. The passage certainly qualifies as a mystical union between God and humanity.

Therefore, the earliest written records of the NT and of Jesus is the witness of a mystic. It not only records Jesus' earthy life and ministry but also the

---

[25] *Ibid.*, 114.
[26] Inge, *Christian Mysticism*, 67.

impact of the transfiguring experience and its continued presence in the life of Paul/Saul who never met Jesus in the flesh.[27] Even though there is no evidence that Paul/Saul had ever met Jesus there was at least some common knowledge as to who Jesus said he was and his ministry. However, as recorded in the Book of Acts Paul/Saul did not recognize Jesus as the person in his vision but would have known the name.

> As he journeyed, he came near Damascus, and suddenly a light shone around him from heaven. Then he fell to the ground, and heard a voice saying to him, "Saul, Saul, why are you persecuting Me?" And he said, "Who are You, Lord?" Then the Lord said, "I am Jesus, whom you are persecuting. It *is* hard for you to kick against the goads." So, he, trembling and astonished, said, "Lord, what do You want me to do?" Then the Lord *said* to him, "Arise and go into the city, and you will be told what you must do." And the men who journeyed with him stood speechless, hearing a voice but seeing no one. Then Saul arose from the ground, and

---

[27] Underhill, *The Mystics of the Church*, 29.

> when his eyes were opened, he saw no one.
> But they led him by the hand and
> brought *him* into Damascus. And he was
> three days without sight, and neither ate nor
> drank.[28]

It was the union between Saul/Paul and God in a mystical sense that transformed him into a believer, the change did not come from a cognitive knowledge of the story but from a spiritual recognition and interaction with Jesus as Lord.

Christian mysticism derived from the truth of the Bible and the experiences of those who follow Christ. Many will say however that Christian mysticism is philosophically based upon Neoplatonism[29] and that the entire structure of Christian Mysticism was borrowed. Secular philosophers proffered that Christian authors writing of the spiritual life and its various stages, merely copied which had been developed by Greek philosophers. Certainly, Christianity was influenced by the Greek philosophers, it is widely known that Plotinus, a Neoplatonist, had a great effect on Augustine.[30]

---

[28] Acts 9:3-9, NKJV

[29] The belief that human perfection and happiness is achievable without awaiting an afterlife. Perfection and happiness used synonymously could be achieved through philosophical contemplation.

[30] Underhill, *The Mystics of the Church*, 60.

The three stages of Christian Mysticism (purgation, illumination, and union) are expressions that are similar, to and borrowed from the Neoplatonists. Many Christian scholars see that the Neoplatonists merely labeled and categorized that which could have been easily developed from the mystical experiences from Isaiah. As compared to Neoplatonism (Plato 427 BCE[31]) Biblical mysticism can be traced to the Abraham in the Book of Genesis (roughly 2000 BCE[32]) to present day Christian mystics.

The three stages of the mystical way for the Christian mystic are described as a journey of awareness. It does not describe a philosophic experience or a neat category of religious experience; but it is the aim of life that wants nothing less than union with God.[33]

Purgation or Purgative Life is seen as a process where the mystic detached themselves from their life, seen at times as confession, self-mortification or in the idea of detachment or asceticism; philosophically the death of the ego.[34] Plato felt that it consisted of the separation of the soul as much as possible from the body and concentrating on the

---

[31] David Wallenchinsky and Irving Wallace, *The People's Almanac*, (Garden City, New York: Doubleday and Co., Inc. 1975) 1418.

[32] Barbara Smith, *The Westminster Concise Bible Dictionary*, (Philadelphia: Westminster Press, 1075) 17.

[33] Underhill, *The Mystics of the Church*, 20.

[34] Cox, *Handbook of Christian Spirituality*, 28.

soul, by the soul, in such a way that it was freed from the shackles of the body.[35] In the Christian sense it is seen more as a purification and consecration of character, and a separation from material and carnal interest.[36] Christian purification includes self-discipline and a certain degree of austere simplicity and suffering, but not of necessity a maltreatment of the body.[37]

Purgation has been described by St. John of the Cross as "the gradual spiritualization of mystic's prayer, especially the painful struggles and obscurities which accompany the transition from the stage of meditation on religious themes and figures to the beginning of real contemplation."[38] In some aspects the purification process is perpetual, never ending yet moving slowly toward completion. This is what is meant by mystical authors when they write about the "Way of Purification" being a slow and painful completion to conversion.[39] What is being described here is the radical shift of the self from worldly and physical pleasure and all that is associated with the temporal and mortal to being turned toward the heavenly, spiritual and all that is associated with the immortal and eternal. "The essence of purgation is the self-simplification. . .nothing can happen till the involved interest and

---

[35] *Ibid.*, 29.
[36] Underhill, *The Mystics of the Church*, 26.
[37] Inge, *Christian Mysticism*, 11.
[38] *Ibid.*, 26, 27.
[39] Underhill, *Mysticism: A Study*, 204.

tangled motives of the self are simplified. . .recognized and cast away."[40] Summed up, the nature of purgation is being "sold out" and radically changed for God; not just a superficial change rather a change where the mystic goes through an inspection and introspection in every facet of life and nature. A shift that realizes some aspects of life will change drastically forever, and other aspects may seem completely untouched. The process starts with faith, ends in trust and consecration, and a purification of mind, soul, and body aligned with God.

Illumination is the next stage in the mystic way and is a "somewhat misleading term involving mystical faith; requires one to concentrate all of one's facilities on God"[41] Underhill called it a "peaceful certitude of God and a perception of true values of existence in his light."[42] The reality is that the mystic receives a peek at what of the glory of God really is after they have suffered and have been through anguish. They find that their God is wonderful and majestic God, one who has splendid prospects opening to those who remain faithful.[43] It is for those "who have permitted God to seize and sanctify [them] to the full measure and power of

---

[40] *Ibid.*

[41] Tuttle, Jr. *Mysticism in the Wesleyan Tradition*, 24.

[42] Underhill, *The Mystics of the Church*, 27.

[43] Sister Rose Aquin Caimana, PhD, *Mysticism in Gabriela Mistral* (Bew York: Pageant Press International Corp., 1969), 62.

[His] grace."[44] The illuminative life begins in the concentration of the mystic's entire substance upon God. "It differs from the purgative life, not in discarding good works, but in having come to perform them no longer as virtues. . .[but]. . .willingly and almost spontaneously."[45] As mystics progress in the mystic way they progress in what's called spiritual refinement. They reach the heights of contemplation where existence, the world, and everything is not a problem but a mystery.[46] The mystic however is still not yet involved with the supreme communion with God, they have merely passed through the preliminaries. They have detached themselves from their major entanglements; reordered their life in such a way that they have a certitude about God and their soul in relation to God.[47] They have become self-disciplined with an outward life and simplicity.

The actual illumination process may come in different experiences, described as "shafts of light into the soul."[48] When investigating the mystical way three main experiences are discovered. One experience is what is referred to as a joyous expectation of God. "The ascetic writers called it the 'practice in the presence of God' . . .not to be confused with a unique consciousness of union with

---

44 *Ibid.*
45 Inge, *Christian Mysticism*, 12.
46 Cox, *Handbook of Christian Spirituality*, 31.
47 Underhill, *Mysticism: A Study*, 234.
48 Tuttle, *Mysticism in the Wesleyan Tradition*, 25.

29

the divine."[49] The mystic is not absorbed in a oneness, but is able to meditate on God in a closer way. Illumination can be thought of as a spiritual engagement, but not yet a marriage.[50]

Another experience of illumination deals with the mystics' perception and world view. Their human perceptions seem heightened and daily matters and circumstances take on an enhanced awareness. It seems as though the "doors of perception have been cleansed.[51]

An additional mystic experience is an extension of consciousness and an increase in various degree of the mystics' intuitional or transcendental self. It is through this type of experience that we achieve illumination through visions, dreams, possession, meditations, pure contemplation, immanence, artistic expression and active prayer and conversation with God.[52]

Illumination can appear by any one or all of these experiences. Some manifestations seem to be more dominant than others and for the Christian they feel some experiences would not be used by God. For the Christian Godly illumination seems always divinely initiated and inspired with God as the author of true illumination as God is the aim of purgation. It appears that purgation and illumination interact together drawing the mystic nearer to the

---

[49] Underhill, *Mysticism: A Study*, 240.
[50] *Ibid.*
[51] *Ibid.*
[52] *Ibid.*

perfect so that they seemingly dove-tail together. The mystic is compelled forward searching for a special union with God. This moves the mystic to a knowledge where the concept that a union with God is completely possible and preferable. The transition to union is not as straight forward as the progression from purgation to illumination.

There is a dark divide between illumination and union, a time when "God withdraws. . .forcing mystics to come to God by naked faith."[53] This dark divide is a period of emptiness and stagnation so far as mystical activity is concerned.[54] St. John of the Cross called this period the "Dark Night of the Soul," dark because no indisputable vision occurs.[55] At times it seems that nothing can be discerned, nothing "seen, smelled, or heard as in a distinct visions and senses or imagination,"[56] "The soul passes from the life of senses to the life of the spirit, an undertaking that demands effort and consistency and a deep unquestioning faith. . . That is what Sister Rose Aquin Caimana calls the route of the 'la noche oscura del alma;' the dark night of the soul."[57]

---

[53] Tuttle, *Mysticism in the Wesleyan Tradition*, 25.
[54] Underhill, *Mysticism: A Study*, 381.
[55] St. John of the Cross, *Ascent of Mount Carmel* (1580), ed. E. Alison Peers (Garden City, New York: Image Books, 1958), 82.
[56] Louis Dupré, *The Deeper Life: An Introduction to Christian Mysticism*, (New York: Crossroad Publishing, 1981), 82.
[57] Sister Caimana, *Mysticism in Gabriela Mistra*, 61.

The Dark Night of the Soul. . .puts the sensory spiritual appetites to sleep, deadens them, and deprives them of the ability to find pleasure in anything. It binds their imagination and impedes it from doing any good discursive work. It makes the memory cease, the intellect becomes dark and unable to understand anything, and hence it causes the will to become arid and constrained, and all the faculties empty and useless. And over this hangs a dense and burdensome cloud which afflicts the soul, and keeps it withdrawn from the good[58]

The Dark Night of the Soul begins with our intellect and the experiencing of drastic change. Purgation is the purifying element of this process. The mystic is found to have been stripped of all that the world has given. This stripping process is a privation of all desires and complete separation from the material.[59] After purgation the mystic is then illuminated, possibly by divine vision, or premonition, or from a 'divine whisper,' or a recognition of the truth of 'God's Word.' Whatever experience or combination of experiences through which illumination is given the mystic has touched God but is not encased and consumed by God. The

---

[58] Fra. Apfelman, *The Dark Night of the Soul*, In Inner Sanctum Networks [electronic bulletin board] (March 1, 1997), inner-sanctom.com, 1.

[59] Inge, *Christian Mysticism*, 224.

mystic is left in the dark, alone, suffering again but differently. The road they begin to travel is by faith and this darkness is suffering to the intellect.[60] These purifying and strengthening qualities of suffering are well known by scholars.[61] These qualities are realized by those who have suffered but are not perceived by those who are suffering.[62] All those who have suffered, suffered alone in their own private worlds, with no one but the suffering mystic to feel the slings and arrows of their life. Nothing written can adequately describe the loneliness of pain and depression and loss. This is the Dark Night of the Soul, an overflow to the strange mixture and reaction to the purgative and illuminative stages of the "mystic way." At the end of this darkness only one thing is needed, that is to love God.[63]

It must be remembered that the mystic may go through these stages more than once, each time growing deeper and richer in their understanding and union with God.[64] The mystic may have multiple periods of purgation, and then periods of illumination and of course have their share of darkness and also experience union with God.

---

[60] *Ibid.*

[61] Dupré, *The Deeper Life: An Introduction to Christian Mysticism,* 64.

[62] *Ibid.*

[63] Roland H. Bainton, *Here I Stand: A Life of Martin Luther* (Nashville: Abington Press, 1978), 43.

[64] Cox, *Handbook of Christian Spirituality,* 28.

After the Christian mystic passes through the "Dark Night of the Soul" they pass on to the "Unitive Life" also known as the "Contemplative Life." The unitive stage is described as the "ultimate attainment of the mystic way."[65] "The mystic considers this the perfect and self-forgetting harmony of the regenerated will with God," so that the mystics "being" is to God, as the mystic hand is to the mystic.[66] The union is the highest state of bonding a soul can enjoy in its earthly existence. Thinking of this bond in human terms as a marriage, the bonding is more than a betrothal and could be better described as a spiritual marriage, a complete transforming union.[67]

A complete union with God is the ideal of religions, however, Christian scholars see this union as a continuous process that is never attainable in this life. Mystics "must therefore beware of regarding the union as anything more than an infinite process, though at its end is part of the eternal counsel of God, there is a sense in which it is already a fact, and not merely a thing desired."[68] Thomas Merton in *The Silent Life* enlightens us concerning monks, and gives us a glimpse of what the unitive life entails. Merton helps us see the particle side of what is entailed in the illuminative

---

[65] *Ibid.*, 31.
[66] Underhill, *The Mystics of the Church*, 27.
[67] Sister Caimana, *Mysticism in Gabriela Mistra*, 62.
[68] Inge, *Christian Mysticism*, 12.

stage. In his chapter titled *Puritas Cordis* Merton writes:

> We define a monk as a man who leaves everything else in order to seek God, But this definition is not going to mean much unless we also define the search for God. And this is not any easy matters. For God is at the same time, as one of the Fathers said, everywhere and nowhere. How can I find someone who is nowhere? And if I am nowhere, how shall I be able to say that I am still "I"? Will I still rejoice in having found Him? How can I find Him who is everywhere? If He is everywhere, He is indeed close to me, and with me, and in me. . .[69]

As we read over this passage it indicates the unitive life comes from faith. The monk, or we can say, the mystic rejects the worldly and embraces the spiritual as in the purgative stage. When the illuminative stage appears, the mystic is confronted with an influx of information. They are confused as in dark night of the soul before the realization of the closeness of God. How does this closeness come to the mystic? It comes through faith in God. Merton's writing and description of the monk hints at the

---

[69] Thomas Merton, *The Silent Life*, (New York: Dell Publishing Co., Inc., 1956), 17.

unitive stage and that it is accomplished by faith. The faith referred to is the "proximate and proportionate means whereby the soul is united with God; for such is the likeness between itself and God that there is no other difference, save that which exists between seeing God and believing in Him. For, even as God is infinite, so faith sets Him before us as infinite. . ."[70]

Thomas á Kempis in his writing *The Imitation of Christ* gives insight to the spiritual aspect of the unitive stage. Kempis shows us how the devout soul should, with all its heart be united to Christ.[71]

> O Lord, grant that I may find You and open my heart to You so that I may find joy with You. . .May we speak to one another as two friends. . .I pray. . .that I may be united to You and take my heart from the loves of the world so that I may learn Your eternal and heavenly ways. . . when. . .I will entirely forget myself. You in me and I am in You and so together may we dwell. . . You show Your love without measure. . .I can give You nothing that would be more acceptable to You but myself. And when my soul is perfectly united with You my heart will rejoice. . .[72]

[70] St. John of the Cross, *Ascent of Mount Carmel*, 114.
[71] Thomas á Kempis, *The Imitation of Christ*, (1450) ed. Giles Barton (New York: Guidance House, 1942), 85.
[72] *Ibid.*

Kempis' words bring different facets of Christian mysticism into focus. The passage gives us a glimpse into the unitive life with God, a union that for the mystic is one of love and immersion into the divine will. A union of faith, that has a spiritual significance along with a practical one.

Kempis' passage also points out that Christian mysticism has two distinct yet basic foci. Mentioned previously these are Theocentric and Christocentric contemplation. Thomas á Kempis writings would be considered Christocentric as opposed to the Theocentric contemplation of Saint Augustine.

Although mysticism typically requires, and mystics usually practice, an austere lifestyle they do not practice legalism. Legalism is in a different paradigm than mysticism, much as someone adheres to Platonism or Aristotelianism. Legalism and mysticism cannot exist together, a person is either one or the other. The legalist has the concept of God as a righteous judge but a judge none-the-less. They see God as the great task-master of the vineyard that the Christian labors in: the Gospel as the "new law of the age," and the sanction of duty as a categorical essential.[73] The legalist sees life as a brutal slavery, they have concentrated on the process and have little regard for the goal. We get a working definition of *Legalism* within Christianity typically

---

[73] Inge, *Christian Mysticism*, 36.

by implying salvation is by works instead of grace. There is another understanding by some where their distinctive accepts salvation by grace but codifies behavior by rigid rules of conduct.[74] However, the Christian mystic is not dealing with hard and fast rules, in whose relentlessness we find only despair.[75]

The Christian mystic relies and trusts only in God and the union they are trying to attain is a process that is ever rushing toward completion, yet never achieving all that is possible. It is a time when God and the mystic touch in perfect love. "In Michelangelo's fresco on the vault on the Sistine Chapel, Adam's outstretched hand has just been released from the divine finger, and an empty space has begun to separate the two. The mystic knows that the hand and finger continue to touch in a common space."[76] This is the mystical union God and the mystic touching.

---

[74] Irving Hexman, *Concise Dictionary of Religion*, (Downers Grove, Illinois: Intervarsity Press, 1993), 135.

[75] Francis J. McConnell, *John Wesley*, (New York: Abingdon Press, 1939), 63.

[76] Dupré, *The Deeper Life: An Introduction to Christian Mysticism*, 25.

Chapter 2 - The Mystics in John Wesley's Life

Any information or biographies about John Wesley always has a section concerning Wesley and mysticism. These book chapters and sections may not be titled in that way, but they deal with the general thrust of Wesley and mysticism. There is no doubt that Wesley knew the mystic writers well and condensed many of their writings. This collection included the writings of such mystics as John of Avila, Bourignon, de Renty, Fénelon, Madam Guyon, Jacob Boehm, William Law and Thomas á Kempis. Wesley considered that many of the Christian mystical beliefs, as well as the traditional doctrinal divisions of the church shared a common legacy concerning the holiness of God. He understood that this legacy could be traced through Ignatius of Loyola, to Thomas á Kempis to the leaders of the early church.[77]

Wesley was familiar with the various systems of mysticism and was knowledgeable about Roman Catholic mysticism as well as Jansenism, Quietism, and the various protestant mystics of the period. As for Wesley's own personal mysticism it had a distinctly Roman Catholic flavor. Of the Roman

---

[77] Richard P. Heitzenrater, *Wesley and the people Called Methodist*, (Nashville: Abington Press, 1995), 321.

Catholics Wesley read and condensed the most common were post-Reformation mystics.[78]

Wesley's knowledge of Roman Catholic traditions and mystics is displayed in his second letter to Bishop Lavington in 1750 where Wesley said he had gradually put on a more Catholic spirit.[79] Although he never converted to "popery,"[80] he was well versed with Catholic doctrine, their mystics and contemplative life.[81] Contemplative theology, both Christocentric and Theocentric has always been a strong tradition in Roman Catholic and Anglican churches. This mystic spirituality emphasizes a deeper spiritual life with the goal of direct union with God through the spiritual disciple of prayer, meditation and fasting.[82]

The major objection Wesley had to the doctrine of good works in the Catholic church was his thought that good works could not be done before justification.[83] However, Wesley looked at the mystics of the Catholic church differently. Catholic mystics span a time frame that reached from the very beginning of the Holy Catholic Church to the

---

[78] Tuttle, *Mysticism in the Wesleyan Tradition*, 25, 26.

[79] John Wesley, *Works, vol V*, (Bristol: printed by William Pine, 1771), 400.

[80] Francis J. McConnel, *John Wesley*, (New York: Abingdon Press, 1939), 111.

[81] V.H.H. Green, *John Wesley*, (London: Thomas Nelson and Sons, Ltd., 1964), 20.

[82] Daniel Reid, ed. *Dictionary of Christianity in America*, (Dowers Grove, Illinois: Intervarsity Press, 1990), 492.

[83] Wesley, *Works, vol. I*, 218,221.

Roman Catholic Church to the post-Reformation era. The mysticism of the Roman Catholic Church especially since the Reformation had provided an extraordinary continuity of piety and devotion to God.[84] Robert Tuttle in his book *Mysticism in the Wesleyan Tradition* states that the after the Reformation Catholic mysticism tended to follow two trends:

> One trend continued along the lines of medieval mysticism, which, in an effort to counterbalance formalism in the church had lost the perspective of its already unstable synthesis between Christian Dogma and neo-platonic thought. A second trend, however, centered in Spain and France and usually [was] associated with the so-called Counter Reformation. . ."[85]

Of the many Catholic mystics Wesley read the majority of the second type.[86] Many were connected to the Counter-Reformation in either Spain, France, or Germany. These included people such as Lorenzo Scupoli, Cardinal Fénelon, Marquise De Renty, Thomas á Kempis, John of Avila, and Gregory Lopez. Each of these mystics had a great impact on Wesley's life and theology.

---

[84] William James, *Varieties of religious Experience*, (New York: Longmans, Green, 1919), 406.
[85] Tuttle, *Mysticism in the Wesleyan Tradition*, 26.
[86] Green, *John Wesley*, 21,22.

Lorenzo Scupoli, author of *Pugna Spiritualis* (*Spiritual Combat*) held a special place in Wesley's thinking as did with his mother Susanna's.[87] Scupoli saw the spiritual life as a type of holy war where he writes:

. . .addressing the understanding and the will. [he] argues that a man must hate himself and renounce his own ego, and turn with a wholehearted love to God. . .the essential factor of Christian obedience. . .the readiness to accept suffering and temptation. . .[88]

This is a recurring theme in Wesley's doctrine and writings, the idea of renouncing self and turning ourselves over entirely to God. Looking at this example we can see the significant impact these ideas had on Wesley's life especially since he was one of his mother's favorite authors. Susanna Wesley recommended a number of other mystic authors to her son. However, it was in Scupoli's writings that she found the "summons to continue the struggle for Christian perfection and to withdraw from the things of this world."[89] Another author she recommended to her son was the writings of Thomas á Kempis.

---

[87] Robert G. Tuttle, *John Wesley: His Life and Theology*, (Grand Rapids, Michigan: Zondervan Publishing House, 1978) 48.
[88] *Ibid.*
[89] *Ibid.*

Thomas á Kempis (1380-1471) was originally born Thomas Hämerken at Kempden near Düsseldorf, Germany. He entered the cloister in 1399 and in 1413 he was ordained a priest, spending most of his time copying scripture and devotional text.[90] Kempis authored a number of books that included *Prayers and Meditations of the Life of Christ, The Elevation of the Mind, The Soliloquy of the Soul, On Solitude and Silence, On the Discipline of the Cloister,* and *The Imitation of Christ.* The last monograph was of particular interest to both Susanna and John Wesley. It is written that John Wesley "at the age 22, through reading Thomas á Kempis. . . began to see, that the true religion was seated in the heart, and that God's law extended to our thoughts as well as our words and actions."[91]

Cardinal Fénelon was another who had an impact on Wesley's view of 'pure love.' Wesley had heard of Fénelon by the Winter of 1726 and by February of 1727 he was transcribing Fénelon's *Discourse on Simplicity.* When Wesley read Fénelon's *"The Christian Library,* one [he] concludes that it could just as easily be called a discourse on Christian perfection."[92] A discussion

---

[90] Cox, *Handbook of Christian Spirituality*, 122, 123.

[91] Gregory S. Clapper, *John Wesley on Religious Affections: His Views on Experience and Emotion and their Role in Christian Life and Theology*, (Metuchen, New Jersey: The Scarecrow Press, Inc., 1989), 128.

[92] Tuttle, *Mysticism in the Wesleyan Tradition*, 153.

concerning Fénelon's doctrine of pure love could be described as "the love which God has for us which gives us everything; but the greatest gift that He can give us is the love that we ought to have for Him."[93] Fénelon' stated that there were five kinds of love that a mystic would experience as he went through each stage of the mystic way. He writes:

.(i) purely servile – the love of God's gifts apart from Himself;
(ii) the love of mere covetousness, which regards the love of God only as the condition off happiness;
(iii) that of hope, in which, the desire for our own welfare is still predominant;
(iv) interested love, which is still mixed with self-regarding motives;
(v) disinterested love. . . In the purgative life love is mixed with fear of hell; in the illuminative with the hope of heaven, while in the highest stage we are united to God in the peaceable exercise of pure over. .[94]

John Wesley saw perfection as a type of pure or perfect love, a love where we have given our all to Christ, holding nothing back. Wesley wrote:

Let your soul be so filled with so entire a love to him that you may love nothing but for His sake. Have a pure intention of heart, a steadfast regard for

---

[93] Olive Wyon, *Desire for God*, (London: Fontana, 1966) 34.
[94] Inge, *Christian Mysticism*, 236.

glory in all your actions. For then . . . is that mind in us that was also in Christ Jesus . . .[95]

Wesley was impacted by what Fénelon had to say about love. He especially favored Fenelon's concept of simplicity of love which was "that grace which frees the soul from all unnecessary reflections upon itself."[96]

Marquis de Renty was a French mystic whose life of piety and faith also inspired Wesley.[97] Wesley was impressed by de Renty's holiness, temperance, and service to God, feeling that de Renty outlined the ideal Christian life.[98] Wesley had a great deal of respect and admiration for him and knew that like himself de Renty had read Thomas á Kempis at an early age and was affected positively by the experience.[99] "Wesley expresses few open criticisms of de Renty's life, and de Renty's area of influence on Wesley runs wider and deeper than any other mystic. In fact, Wesley even defended de Renty from his critics."[100] Wesley did not concur with all of de Renty's thoughts, some of his ideas never figuring greatly in Wesley's life of contemplation. However, there is no doubt that de

---

[95] John Wesley, *A Plain Account of Christian Perfection* ([(1777) ed. Thomas Jackson (1872)] ed. George Lyons, (Nampa, ID: Northwest Nazarene College, 1996)), 2.; Inge, *Christian Mysticism*, 67.

[96] John Wesley, *The Letters of John Wesley, vol VI*, ed. John Telford, (London: Epworth, 1931), 128.

[97] Heitzenrater, *Wesley and the people Called Methodist*, 73.

[98] Wesley, *The Letters of John Wesley, vol VIII*, 171.

[99] *Ibid.*, 190.

[100] Tuttle, *Mysticism in the Wesleyan Tradition*, 92.

Renty has a strong affect on Wesley and gave him an example of "living in the world, and yet dying to it."[101]

John of Avila (Juan de Avila), known as the apostle of Andalusia, was born in a small city in the province of Toledo around 1500. He was a great preacher and because of envy, spent a short time imprisoned by the Inquisition.[102] John of Avila had an early association with Jesuits and did a number of things to further their work in Spain. He was also the one who spread the spirit of the Catholic counter-Reformation from the Jesuits, to the Carmelites. John of Avila's written works are well known and include *Audi Filia*, a book on perfection and his spiritual letters. Extracts of these letters were found in Wesley's *Christian Library*.[103]

The Spanish mystics were instrumental in the spreading of the Counter-Reformation and its associated mysticism. As previously mentioned, John of Avila was responsible for the spread of mysticism from the Jesuits to the Carmelites and was also St. Teresa of Avila's mentor who in turn mentored and counseled St. John of the Cross.

St. Teresa of Avila was a Spanish mystic and Carmelite nun of the 1600's. and wrote *The Way of Perfection* to instruct her "daughters to love prayer,

---

[101] *Ibid.*, 93.
[102] Rev, John M'clintock, D.D., and James Strong, S.T.D., *Cyclopædia of Biblical, Theological, and Ecclesiastical Literature vol. IV* (New York: Harper and Brothers Publishers, 1872), 962.
[103] Tuttle, *Mysticism in the Wesleyan Tradition*, 30.

the most effective way of attaining virtue."[104] She writes, " I shall speak of nothing of which I have no experience, either in my own life or in the observations of others, or which the Lord has not taught ne in prayer,"[105] St. Teresa writes about the separation from the materialism of society and drawing closer to, and contemplating upon the truths of God. She was interested in evaluating the return of affection we give and realizing what is important and what is not. This detachment was not just from the material things of the world but even from our own selves.[106] St. Teresa of Avila was a mystic that practiced selectivity, believing in being selective about what someone did or did not do in life. She influenced the life of an old Order and brought it back "to its duty of direct communion with a transcendental world.[107] Although Wesley never mentioned St. Teresa or St. John of the Cross it was their type of mysticism that deeply affected the mystics of the Counter-reformation. Wesley investigated Counter-Reformation mystics and it was these mystics who were the 'meat' that Wesley condensed.[108]

John of Avila additionally influenced Gregory Lopez, missionary to Mexico, who practiced obedience to God, self-denial, and lived in the

---

[104] St. Teresa of Avila. *The Way of Perfection* (1565) ed. E. Alison Peers (Garden City, New York: Image Books, 1964), 14.
[105] *Ibid.*, 34, 35.
[106] *Ibid.*, 88.
[107] Underhill, *Mysticism: A Study*, 468.
[108] Tuttle, *Mysticism in the Wesleyan Tradition*, 31.

continual presence of God.[109] At the age of twenty he went to Mexico from Spain and there he became a missionary to the Indians. Wesley saw himself in somewhat the same way as Lopez saw himself. At the time he was going to Georgia and he relied a great deal on Lopez's life as a guide for his own. Lopez went to Mexico to work with the Indians and have unbroken communion with God and Wesley saw himself the same way.[110]

Jansenism and Quietism are two systems, at least in origin, that formed the mystical experience of the Catholic church. Jansenism is named after Cornelius Jansen (ius) who was born in Northern Holland in 1585. During his time in secondary higher education he met a Frenchman, Jean Baptiste Duvergier de Haurannae (St. Cyran). While at the University of Louvain, Jansen and Cyran met those who cherished the doctrine of grace.[111] They found that their beliefs were in general frowned upon by the Roman Catholic church and in particular the Jesuits. Jansen, along with Cyran, had a special interest in Augustine, studying him for five years and reading all he wrote ten times.[112] Jansen made it his life's work to methodically categorize the works of Augustine. The categories included the grace of God, the condition of fallen man, free will, original sin, and points that aim towards spiritual renewal in the Catholic Church. Even though Wesley did not

---

[109] Green, *John Wesley, 21.*
[110] Tuttle, *John Wesley: His Life and Theology*, 34.
[111] M'clintock, and Strong, *Cyclopædia of Biblical Literature*, 770, 771.
[112] Tuttle, *Mysticism in the Wesleyan Tradition*, 33.

agree with all of Jansenist doctrine he was upset that the Catholic church smothered "this zeal for genuine piety."[113]

Quietists are said to have implemented the Jansenists' theory.[114] The basis of Quietism is that the soul leaves everything to God, despising all options, even the option of grace. The plan would be that the soul would wait on the Spirit of God, without the use of grace in any way, until the soul and the spirit are at pardon and peace.[115] Some describe "Quietism's acute mental concentration and its suspicion of consolation simply degenerated into an extreme position of complete indifference."[116] Others have called them a cancerous growth upon the healthy body of mysticism[117] and a heresy that warred against the Roman Catholic Church.[118] Wesley wasn't a Quietist but did recommend and publish many of their writings because of their relentless pursuit of Christian perfection.[119]

Mystics from the Roman Catholic church who came from various parts of Europe during the Catholic Counter-Reformation contributed to Wesley's understanding of perfection, self-denial, obedience, and union with God. Although Wesley

[113] John Wesley, *Ecclesiastical History, vol IV,* (London: printed by J. Paramore, 1781), 44.
[114] Ronald Knox, *Enthusiasm,* (Oxford: Clarendon Publ., 1950), 232.
[115] McConnel, *John Wesley,* 79, 80, 139.
[116] Tuttle, *Mysticism in the Wesleyan Tradition,* 40,41.
[117] Knox, *Enthusiasm,* 239.
[118] Underhill, *Mysticism: A Study,* 150.
[119] Tuttle, *Mysticism in the Wesleyan Tradition,* 41.

did not adopt Catholic mysticism in total and actually felt some was misguided yet it gave him a focus point in his search for the truth. Wesley studied the writings of Juan de Castanzia, Magdelen de Pazzi, and Madame Guyon and found the one thing that connected many of the mystics particularly important to him, was their progress in perfect love, the goal of all religion.[120]

Protestant mysticism is as varied in nature and style as are Christian mystics. Within the Protestant Reformation, with its emphasis on personal rather than institutional conviction, mysticism would blossom. In general. This was not the case even though Martin Luther had his mystical side.[121] Luther had read *Theologica Germanica* and was familiar with the beliefs of the German mystics.

Theologica Germanica or *Book of the Perfect Life* was probably written in Frankfort about the year 1350 by a priest in the Teutonic Order. [The Book] One of the most successful of many attempts to make mystic principles available to the common man, this book was greatly loved by Luther. . .[122]

Luther strived to yield himself to God in the mystic way. "At times he was lifted up as if he were amid the choirs of angels. But the sense of alienation would return . . .the dark night of the soul."[123] Luther's mystical tendencies were perplexed when

---

[120] *Ibid*, 42.
[121] Underhill, *The Mystics of the Church*, 212.
[122] *Ibid.*, 212, 464.
[123] Bainton, *Here I Stand*, 43.

he contemplated the inaccessible light in which God dwells. However, dis have a strong unshakable faith in God which was "akin to the *Gelassenhelt* (calmness) of the [German] mystics, an expression of the confidence in the restorative power of God."[124] Unfortunately, the mystical part of the Reformation died in large part with Luther's conversion to *sola fide*. Because of this, mysticism has not played a large part in the Lutheran Church and even a smaller part in the Calvinist branch of the church.[125]

Wesley was influenced by Luther in a number of important ways, most significant by his writings. The most impactful was Luther's *Preface to the Epistle to the Romans*. Wesley was attending a meeting at a Moravian Chapel on Aldersgate Street in London. Someone at the meeting was reading the preface and Wesley had his heart-warming experience. Luther's simple concepts concerning faith and how it changed the heart of the believer. Luther's writings played an important part in the formation of German Pietism and Wesley's conversion.[126] Wesley speaking of the occasion said, "I felt my heart strangely warmed. I felt I did trust in Christ, and Christ alone for salvation: and an assurance was given me, that He had taken away

---

[124] *Ibid.*, 43, 265.

[125] Underhill, *The Mystics of the Church*, 212.

[126] Clarke Garret, *Spirit Possession and Popular Religion: From the Camisards to the Shakers*, (Baltimore: The John Hopkins University Press, 1987), 77, 79.

my sins, even mine, and saved me from the law of sin and death.[127]

Huguenots were another group of mystics that had a substantial impact on Wesley, some of which became known as the French Prophets. Starting around 1560 the Protestant Reformation came to Cévennes in the mountainous region in northern Languedoc, France. From 1630 to 1660 many of these Huguenots altered the manner of their worship and became part of a millennial tradition.[128] Persecution by the Catholic French royalty and Catholics in general drove the Huguenots underground. "Despite surveillance the Huguenots tried to preserve their religious tradition. Accustomed to the family cult, they perpetuated in secret the familiar forms of private worship."[129]

The private underground church that developed was called the "Desert;" a metaphor describing their spiritual desolation and the geographical location of many of their assemblies. The first prophets started to appear in Huguenot assemblies in 1688 and at first were children. From 1562 to 1598 France was experiencing what is known as the French Wars of Religion where Roman Catholics with the permission of the King tried to exterminate the Huguenot threat. There were some who saw this

---

[127] John Wesley, *The Journal of the Rev. John Wesley, vol. I* (1735-1791) ed. Nhehemiah Curnock, (London: Epworth, 1909), 477.

[128] Hillel Schwartz, *The French Prophets: The History of a Millenarian Group in Eighteenth-Century England*, (Berkley: University of California Press, 1948), 11.

[129] *Ibid.* 14.

prosecution as a sign of the Last Days and the prophesying of the children while they slept as pointing to a revelation toward the truth. Within six months the adults began to prophesy too and by 1689 the experience spread to neighboring areas and with it came persecution. Through the 1690's these French Prophets had frequent visions and prophecies conceding plagues and the end of the world.[130]

"Early in 1702 an itinerant band of inspirés and companions had gathered in the mountains of the Cévennes, fugitives from the deadly justice of priests and soldiers."[131] The fugitives gathered together and formed the Camisards who revolted and fought as a religious paramilitary force through 1706. England in 1706 was no stranger to prophecy or millennial speculation. The Camisard prophet Elie Marion arrived and by 1712, after the final uprising in Cévennes, the Camisards and the French Prophets had adherents scattered across England. The French prophets settled in the same areas as early Puritans appealing to a wide variety of people that had similar religious distinctives in the early Eighteenth Century.[132]

Approximately seven months after his Aldersgate experience, January 1739, John Wesley and some of his friends met with Mary Plewitt a female French Prophet. Wesley described the experience writing that he observed her use of convulsion and prophetic inspiration. He

---

[130] *Ibid.*, 17.

[131] *Ibid.*, 22.

[132] *Ibid.*, 37, 154.

experienced other French prophets in Bristol where he again witnessed convulsions and inspirations and disapproved of them. At Weaver's Hall Wesley pointed out their falsehoods in not speaking according to the Law and Testimony and the danger of their enthusiasm.[133] Wesley felt that although the inspiration was from God, they had no authority of themselves. He felt that they tried to attain their ends without the means and going into artificial directions.[134] Because of Wesley's "apprehension of condemning all manifestations of the Spirit false, and loving true Christian enthusiasm, Wesley condemned the French Prophets but often accepted their tenets."[135] Wesley agreed with their piety, and their dissatisfaction with ineffectual orthodox religion along with the Quietist confidence in some flickering internal light.[136]

William Law was another follower of the French Prophet's tenants that Wesley knew. Law was a disciple of the mystic Jacob Boehme and a self-described scientific mind. Law claimed that Newton's Laws were derived from the works of Boehme.[137] Wesley's first knowledge of Law was when he encountered Law's popular work *Christian Perfection*. Law was a profound English religious

---

[133] Wesley, *The Journal of the Rev. John Wesley, vol. II*, 136-137, 180.

[134] Garret, *Spirit Possession and Popular Religion*, 79.

[135] Schwartz, *The French Prophets*, 207.

[136] Wesley, *The Journal of the Rev. John Wesley, vol. II*, 440, 74. and Wesley, *The Journal of the Rev. John Wesley, vol.III*, 49,50.

[137] Schwartz, *The French Prophets*, 242.

author and brilliant stylist whose writings burned with mystic passion.[138] Law also stressed the need for acts of mortification and self-denial for a life of renunciation and rejection of worldly activities. Law felt worldly activities that should be rejected included horse races, masquerades, theater, and world reading.[139] Wesley similarly included a list containing instructions to his early Methodist disciples opposing worldliness and works of the flesh. Law not only reinforced this pattern in Wesley's mind but also introduced Wesley to a number of mystics by giving him a copy of *Theologica Germanica* in the latter half of 1732.[140] That is not to say that Law introduced mysticism to Wesley rather that he accelerated his interest in it. "Not only did the mystical pursuit of holiness [by Law] appeal to his [Wesley] innate sense of morality, but love of contemplation also appealed to his natural inclination to solitude."[141] Law reinvigorated Wesley's wavering interest in mysticism and the interior life. Wesley's in his *Letters* writes that he recalls Law stating, "I was once a kind of oracle to Mr. Wesley."[142]

Wesley and Law were not the only ones interested in the French Prophets. Peter Böhler, who helped Wesley organize the Fetter Lane Society also found them religiously substantial. The Fetter Lane

---

[138] Underhill, *Mysticism: A Study*, 473.

[139] Green, *John Wesley*, 25,26.

[140] Heitzenrater, *Wesley and the people Called Methodist*, 53 footnote 60.

[141] Tuttle, *Mysticism in the Wesleyan Tradition*, 69.

[142] Wesley, *The Letters of John Wesley, vol IV*, 105.

Society was originally a group of men who would meet holding the religious beliefs and distinctives of the Methodist and Moravian sects yet still follow the Church of England's doctrine. The society's agenda was soteriological based examining each other's spiritual health, The organization eventually grew to include women.[143]

Böhler met Wesley on February 7, 1738 when he immediately diagnosed Wesley's spiritual need.[144] It was a week after Wesley returned from America when he met the German Lutheran minister Böhler. Mysticism was the common denominator between the two with them wanting to achieve the same type of spiritual perfection, however they had different means of achieving their goals. Both Böhler and Wesley as did the mystics emphasized Holiness. The difference was that Böhler saw Holiness as the fruit of faith not the cause. He accented the path of Justification more than the final outcome of Sanctification.[145] Because Böhler had experienced instantaneous conversion he was received into the Moravian Brotherhood and was ordained into the order by their nominal leader Count Zinzendorf (Nikolaus Ludwig, Reichsgraf von Zinzendorf und Pottendorf). Böhler told Wesley that he needed to purge his philosophy. In other words, Wesley was to repudiate natural theology and any idea that God comes from human reason

---

[143] Tuttle, *Mysticism in the Wesleyan Tradition*, 104.
[144] *Ibid.*
[145] Heitzenrater, *Wesley and the people Called Methodist*, 77, 104.

rather than from revelation through Christ.[146] Böhler had been searching for assurance of faith and found it in Moravian distinctiveness and tried to model personal spiritual renewal. As Böhler and Wesley became better acquainted Böhler found that Wesley had no true faith, not missing in a degree but entirely. Law and Böhler knowing each other; Böhler visited him and Wesley wanting to understand their theologies better.[147] At the meeting it became clear that Böhler and Law had some basic differences. Böhler, a Moravian minister, spoke of faith in Christ whereas Law spoke in terms of philosophical mysticism. Law's advice to Wesley was "renounce yourself and be not impatient,"[148] whereas Böhler's advice was to "strip thyself [Wesley] naked of thy own works and thy own righteousness and fly to Him. For whosoever cometh to Him, He will no wise cast out."[149] The idea of spiritually stripping yourself is the "purgative aspect of the Moravian synthesis" and appealed to Wesley. This idea drew Wesley toward the Moravians even more but still preserving much of Law's mystical tendencies.[150]

The Moravian Brotherhood or more properly called *Bohemian Brethren* was an evangelical church which prospered before the Reformation of the sixteenth century. The Church was decimated at the beginning of the Thirty Years War in

---

[146] Green, *John Wesley*, 54,55.
[147] Tuttle, *Mysticism in the Wesleyan Tradition*, 115.
[148] Wesley, *The Letters of John Wesley, vol II*, 240.
[149] *Ibid.*
[150] Tuttle, *Mysticism in the Wesleyan Tradition*, 115.

Germany.[151] The precursor of the Bohemian Brethren was John Huss. Huss was born in 1367 and educated at the University of Prague becoming Rector in 1403. His later condemnation came not from doctrinal abnormalities but because he threatened the hierarchy of the church. He was an ardent defender of Wycliffe and felt that Popes and Cardinals were unnecessary. Huss was later executed and is considered a martyr in the Bohemian/Moravian church.[152]

The Moravians that John Wesley was in contact with were the resuscitated church of the Ancient Bohemian Brethren. At the close of the Bohemian anti-Reformation in 1627, a remnant of the Brethren hid in Bohemian and Moravia keeping up with their traditions for many years. In 1722, those who were in hiding from persecution reappeared and made their way to places open to their worship. Count Zinzendorf opened his estate to them and between 1722-1729 over three hundred eventually building a community called *Herrnhut*.[153]

John Wesley, writing to his brother Charles, described the community and practices of the believers and his perceptions of them. He wrote how they were musical with numerous choirs for men, women, and unique groups. These choirs were

---

[151] M'clintock, and Strong, *Cyclopædia of Biblical Literature*, 581.
[152] Albert Henry Newman, *A Manual of Church History, vol. I,* (Chicago: The American Baptist Publication Society, 1947), 613, 615.
[153] M'clintock, and Strong, *Cyclopædia of Biblical Literature*, 585.

broken into groups of five to seven people. They would meet weekly to exchange religious experiences, pray for each other, stimulate each other's faith, read the bible, and sing hymns.[154] There was one aspect of the Moravians that Wesley didn't understand, the Moravian Synthesis.

Moravian Synthesis can be understood as the promise in assurance of salvation set within a quasi-mystical context based on Christ. The Moravians nurtured the Quietist approach to grace by shunning the formalization of worship and a minimization of external works of righteousness. The major difference between the Moravians and Quietists, apart from the question of atonement was the area of assurance. The Moravians appreciated a peace of mind through confidence that the believer lived in God's approval while the Quietist mystic chose to remain ignorant of his acceptance with God.[155]

Wesley was at first drawn to the Moravians because of their doctrine of assurance however he soon became dissatisfied with his Moravian associates. This came about because of incidents at the Fetter Lane Society over the Moravian distinctive of "Stillness."[156] Wesley felt that this denied the divine ordinances of the Church of England as a proper means to salvation. Additionally, Wesley deplored the fact the Moravians rejected self-denial and the daily cross.[157]

---

[154] Green, *John Wesley*, 65.
[155] Tuttle, *John Wesley: His Life and Theology*, 223.
[156] Tuttle, *Mysticism in the Wesleyan Tradition*, 111 notes.
[157] Garret, *Spirit Possession and Popular Religion*, 89.

In September 1741 Wesley and Zinzendorf had a conversation concerning their religious similarities and differences. Zinzendorf felt that Wesley's attitude was legalistic with a legalistic view of holiness.[158] Wesley recorded Zinzendorf's thoughts in his journal where he quotes Zinzendorf saying, "We [Moravians] spit out all self-denial; we tread it underfoot. As believers, we do everything that we wish and nothing beyond. No purification precedes perfect love."[159] For Wesley the final break came in 1740 when twenty-five men and nearly all the women who had belonged to the Fetter Lane Society joined Wesley's new society that was meeting at Moorfield's old Cannon Foundry.[160]

The Moravians added a great deal to Wesley's understanding of assurance. Wesley found their mystical tendencies to be tantalizing compared to his own mystical proclivities asserting a 'new' doctrine within a familiar understanding.[161] Nevertheless, the Moravians also showed Wesley the seeming emptiness of mysticism and still they gave Wesley the one thing he had looked for but couldn't find anywhere else; assurance. Wesley could just not agree with the idea of Moravian mystical Quietism incorporated in their doctrine. In his journal Wesley writes on November 1, 1739 condemning the idea of not doing any good works. Even though the Moravian doctrine's appeal was

---

[158] Harold Linström, *Wesley and Sanctification*, (New York: Abington Press, 1946), 138.
[159] Wesley, *The Journal of the Rev. John Wesley, vol. II*, 490.
[160] Garret, *Spirit Possession and Popular Religion*, 90.
[161] Tuttle, *John Wesley: His Life and Theology*, 224.

strong Wesley finally separated from them over the issue.[162]

One of the Protestant mystics that influenced Wesley a great deal, and came late in Wesley's life, was John Fletcher. Fletcher was born and educated in Switzerland and moved to England in 1752. A reader of Thomas á Kempis, Fletcher reacquainted Wesley with the positive aspects of mysticism showing him the significance of continual and courageous self-denial. In the 1770's the Methodist movement was growing however antinomian attitudes (the idea that salvation by faith through the grace of Christ eliminated the need to follow the morals of the Ten Commandments) were starting to be noticed. This antinomian attitude started to spoil the Methodist Circles and Wesley with the help of Fletcher was able to hinder this abuse through the mystic emphasis of Holiness.[163]

Fletcher was able to show Wesley a clear evangelical and scriptural view of mysticism giving him a renewed appreciation of mystical experience. Wesley had a great deal of esteem for Fletcher and wanted him to be his successor. Unfortunately, Fletcher died before that occurred. Wesley felt that in many ways Fletcher's life was a model of a true mystic. Writing about him Wesley said,

I would only observe, that for many years I despaired of finding any inhabitant of Great Britain, that could stand in any degree of comparison with

---

[162] Clapper, *John Wesley on Religious Affections*, 129.
[163] Tuttle, *Mysticism in the Wesleyan Tradition*, 138,139.

61

Gregory Lopez or Monsieur de Renty. But let any impartial person judge if Mr. Fletcher was at all inferior to them. Did he not experience as deep a communion with God, and as high a measure of inward holiness, as experienced by either one or the other of those burning and shining.[164]

Fletcher was influential in many of Wesley's decisions and in changing his views and initiated a new look at mysticism. Wesley knew that there was a unifying focus in mysticism, both in Catholicism and Protestantism in the mystic practice of holy living. He felt a strong kinship with the French Catholic mystics, German mystics, English Calvinist, German Lutheranism, American Revivalists, and Scottish Evangelicals. Wesley believed the previous mentioned groups shared a common heritage that could be traced through Ignatius of Loyola and Thomas á Kempis to the leaders of the early church.[165]

---

[164] Wesley, *Works, vol. XI*, 364.
[165] Heitzenrater, *Wesley and the people Called Methodist*, 320,321.

Fig. 1: John Wesley (left) – Charles Wesley

Fig.2: Thomas á Kempis

Fig. 3: St. Teresa (Teresa of Ávila)

Fig. 4: St. John of the Cross

Fig. 5: Gregory of Nyssa

Fig. 6: Evelyn Underhill

Fig. 7: John M'clintock - James Strong

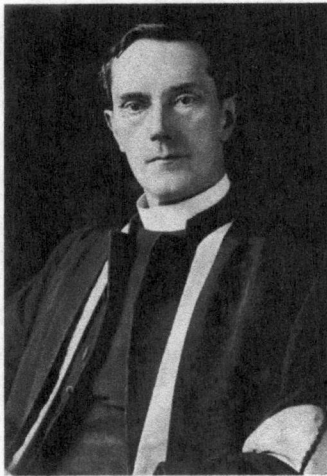

Fig, 8: W. R. Inge

Fig. 9: Donald Metz – Robert Tuttle

Fig. 10: John Wesley's Aldersgate experience as depicted in Elmer T. Clark, *What Happened at Aldersgate* (1938)

Chapter 3 - The Intellectual Interaction Between Thomas á Kempis and John Wesley

Gregory Clapper in his book *John Wesley on Religious Affections* records how Wesley described his early growth in Christianity, "Ay the age of 22, through reading Thomas á Kempis he [Wesley] 'began to see, that true religion was seated in the heart, and that God's law extended to all our thoughts as well as words and actions.'"[166] Such is the affection Wesley had for one of his favorite mystic writers, Thomas á Kempis. It is said that Wesley traveled the countryside of England with Kempis' *Imitation of Christ* in his saddle bag.[167] Wesley saw Kempis as instrumental in propagating and promoting a heritage of holiness within the Christian church.[168] He felt Kempis was "very eminent for piety towards God, reverence for his superiors, and love to his brethren."[169]

Kempis wrote the *Imitation of Christ* in 1445 and even though there has been some controversy

---

[166] Clapper, *John Wesley on Religious Affections*, 128.
[167] Evelyn Underhill, *Man and Supernatural*, (New York: E. P. Dutton & Co., Inc., 1931), 136.
[168] Heitzenrater, *Wesley and the people Called Methodist*, 321.
[169] Wesley, *Works, vol. XIV*, 200.

over his authorship there is significant evidence to support his claim. The book itself was the result of Kempis' ritual of returning to his bedroom nightly and pouring his soul out to God. Wesley found from reading the *Imitation of Christ* that Kempis, by pouring out his soul to God, received a special wisdom that shined in his writings.[170] Other writings Wesley knew were by Kempis were *Prayer and Meditation on the Life of Christ, The Elevation of the Mind, The Soliloquy of the Soul,* and *On Solitude and Silence.*[171]

The *Imitation of* Christ (in Latin *Imitatio Christi*) by Thomas á Kempis is one of the greatest and most enduring of all classic Christian devotional literature, It brings the reader to a testimony of godliness through obedience, setting the tone for personal worship.[172] Each page contains a special admonition to practical mysticism and Christianity in general.

Our Lord said: "he that follows me walks not in darkness." These are the ords of Christ in which we are aught to imitate in his life and manners if we would be truly enlightened and freed from all blindness of heart. Therefore, let our chief study – the study and life of Jesus Christ . . . [173]

---

[170] *Ibid.*

[171] Cox, *Handbook of Christian Spirituality*, 123.

[172] *Ibid.*, 124.

[173] Thomas á Kempis. *The Imitation of Christ* (1450) ed. Giles Barton (New York: Guidance House, 1942), 1.

This work has been called the clearest illustration of Christian mysticism and to some as the "ripe fruit of mediæval Christianity concentrated in the life of the Cloister."[174] Even a cursory reading of the treatise will deeply impact the reader in words that are simple yet powerful. Kempis explores the dynamic divinity of the relationship between God and humanity and forces the person who wants to follow God to decide. The process would include examining their own feelings and recognize their short comings and personal hinderances. However, Kempis isn't promoting legalism but a way to commune with God through Christ. Christian scholars believe Kempis shows truth that can only be seen except in the eyes of eternity.

Son do not believe in your own affections for they are changeable.
As long as you live you will be changeable, even though you try not to be. You will be glad, then sorry, pleased then troubled, devout then undevout, studious then lazy, heavy then light.[175]

A careful examination of Kempis' method of contemplation finds that it was Christocentric and that he used this method almost exclusively in his writings and in his search of the mystic way. His reflections depict almost a proto-Protestantism message of salvation by faith as seen in passages as,

---

[174] Inge, *Christian Mysticism*, 194, 195.
[175] Kempis. *The Imitation of Christ*, 56.

"the teachings of Christ are greater than those of saints and holy men . . ." and "my heart desires to be united with you. You are sufficient unto me."[176] Kempis was interested in Christianity of the heart and preached this heart change, Kempis' mysticism was practical. He saw union with God as not only a life changing experience but a changed life experience with not only the spiritual life of the believer changed but the outward focus too.

The treatise itself is divided into four books/divisions with individual chapters that deal with various subjects. Sections called admonitions deal with both the inner life and the spiritual life. It could be seen as a quest for spiritual understanding and dealing with matters of the soul and the inward speaking of Christ to a faithful believer.[177]

Kempis focused on issues such as avoiding worldly lust and vanity and rejecting vain hope and pride. He taught that Christians should be searching themselves humbly and seeing a true reflection of themselves in the sight of God. Kempis felt the desires of the heart should be examined and moderated being obedient to God, resisting temptations, avoiding rash judgements, and being deliberate in actions. Overall, it means consciously deciding to remain with God and remember the blessing received. Kemps writes,

Son, he who leaves the path of obedience, leaves the path to God's grace. He who desires to have things

---

[176] *Ibid.*, 1, 78.
[177] *Ibid.*, 34.

his own way, loses those things that are all men's. He who does not gladly and freely submit himself to God shows that he does not control himself. Therefore, you must learn to obey your God quickly if you want your body to obey you. The greatest enemy of your soul is yourself when you are not in harmony with your spirit.[178]

The practical advice given here by Kempis is how the believer can walk the mystical-holy walk of Christ. Their walk isn't judged on distance or swiftness but on quality. The walk of the believer is based on denying themselves and following Christ. We can see this in Kempis' prayers that include subjects such as doing the will of God, cleansing the believer's heart and receiving heavenly wisdom.

Most kind Jesus . . . Permit me to do your will and to desire that which is most acceptable to you and most dearly pleases you. Your will be my will, and may my will ever follow Your and agree with it in many ways. Be there in me one wish with you, and let not wish anything but that which you wish. . .[179]

Another subject addressed in Kempis' treatise is purity and the ultimate goal of perfection. He deals with the ability to attain purity in the believer's heart and the perfection of God. From

---

[178] *Ibid.*, 42,43.
[179] *Ibid.*, 44.

Kempis' point of view the believer's purity is not the same as the purity of God. The treatise is concerned with the purity obtained through Christ. Kempis is saying, you have salvation, I have purity, show your salvation without your purity and I will show you my salvation by my purity. Kempis could not understand how one could be living for Christ and yet living as though in the world; he felt one was exclusive of another. This is stated in a number of places in his writings.

A man is raised from earthly things with two wings, they are simplicity and purity. Simplicity should be in your intention, purity in your affection . . . If there is any joy in this world the man with a pure heart has it, and if there is in any place trouble and anxiety and an idle conscience knows it best. . . temptations are often necessary to us even though they are serious and troublesome. Through them we are humbled, purified, and educated- There is one thing that holds back many from learning and improving, fear of difficulty and the labor of trying or fighting. Those who strive most to overcome the things that hold manyback will grow in virtue . . . if you give yourself to fervor you shall find peace and you shall find your tasks lighter for the grace of God and love of virtue. There is more work in resisting vices and passions than to sweat in physical labor. . . Confirm me God by you grace and strengthen my inward virtue. Empty my heart of all that holds me back. Keep me from vile desires . .

. Forsake yourself and you shall find great peace. Give everything, seek nothing, ask nothing, be pure and do not doubt me and you shall have me.[180]

Although many found the *Imitation of Christ* an enduring Christian classic, just as many were not fond of the writing feeling if Kempis' treatise were followed the world would be a terrible place. "There would be no manhood, no love, no tender ties of mother and child, no use of intellect, no trade or science – a set of selfish beings crawling about, avoiding one another."[181] John Wesley didn't feel that way, he felt completely different.

John Wesley edited and revised a number of works from various mystic authors. His practice was to go through numerous times, give a short history of the author, overview of the work itself, and then write a commentary. One of these works included in Wesley's *Christian Library* was Kempis' the *Imitation of Christ*. *The Christian Library* is a fifty-volume work that contains various summaries, anthologies, and commentaries.[182]

In reviewing *The Imitation of Christ* Wesley starts by reviewing Kempis' life, including his origins, family history, his individual history in the monastery. Wesley writes about Kempis' older brother's, Priorship. When looking at Kempis'

---

180 *Ibid.*, 8,20,21,24,53,58.
181 Cox, *Handbook of Christian Spirituality*, 125, 126.
182 Wesley, *Works, vol. XIV*, 200.

character in monastic life and discussing the various monasteries where he served Wesley found Kempis had "piety toward God and reverence for his superiors. [He was] cheerful, patient under affliction, gentle in bearing and kind."[183] Wesley ends with his death in 1471.

After reviewing Kempis' background Wesley looks at his treatise and describes it as plain, simple, unadorned, yet goes on to say that the treatise words have strength, weight, and spirit. Wesley felt that any serious student of the Bible would never tire reading the work through. The general principles are like fruit waiting to be read, devoured, and transformed into a ready source of meditation.[184]

As Wesley studied and meditated on Kempis' treatise, he found levels of encouragement and teaching and discovered hidden within the treatise an almost divine set of virtues. He saw the *Imitation of Christ* as a comprehensive work on Christian perfection. Wesley believed that Kempis had reduced Christian perfection down to three fundamentals: the essence of Christian perfection, the ways and degrees by which it is attained, and the means or mechanisms of it.[185]

Wesley studying the essence of Christian perfection found it was bound to Kempis' perfect love which included the idea of humility. Christian

---

[183] *Ibid.*, 201
[184] *Ibid.*, 202,203.
[185] *Ibid.*

perfection could not be attained without a humble spirit. Wesley further felt that another requirement for Christian perfection is the concept of self-renunciation. The idea of not just self-denial but 'taking up our cross daily.'[186] Kempis writes,

The admonition, 'Deny thyself and take-up your cross and follow me' seems a hard admonition to many people, But it shall be much harder to hear the admonition, 'Go from me, ye cursed people, into everlasting fire.'[187]

Wesley found that Kempis' perfect love not only contained humility and self-renunciation but included unconditional resignation with a union of the believers with the divine will. Unconditional resignation is simply giving one's self over to God completely. Wesley saw this union as the pinnacle of Christian perfection; change the believer from what they were into the imitation of Christ. Wesley believed those who immersed themselves in self-love and love of the world would never achieve Christian perfection.[188]

As Wesley contemplated Kempis' treatise, he felt that it contained stages one would pass through to achieve Christian perfection. Wesley saw these stages as necessary so that the soul would be "fully

---

[186] *Ibid.*
[187] Kempis. *The Imitation of Christ*, 30.
[188] Wesley, *Works, vol. XIV*, 203.

purged from all willful habitual sin; but likewise, that it be enlightened by the knowledge and practice of all virtue, before it can be united to God."[189] There is an obvious similarity between the mystical stages of the mystic way of purgation, illumination, and union and the stages Wesley describes including a type of dark night of the soul. When writing about the right attitude to read Kempis he writes about the advantages it gives to those in Christian warfare. Warfare such as various temptations and moral difficulties in an immoral world.[190] These are situations that believers are expected to pass through while "in the wilderness" before they enter "into the rest of God."[191] When writing about Kempis' treatise, Wesley wrote that it offers encouragement in this time of struggling, for those who desire the practical truth.[192]

Wesley felt the means of Christian perfection were intertwined with the grace of God and included prayer, self-examination, the reading of the scriptures, and holy communion. As Wesley studied Kempis, he found that Kempis' concept of the grace of God as that which takes the human corrupted nature that is prone to evil and heals and strengthens it, allowing the avoidance of sin and the steadily practice of virtue. Prayer wasn't mentioned directly with any enumerated rules in the treatise, but

---

[189] *Ibid.*, 204.
[190] *Ibid.*, 207.
[191] *Ibid.*
[192] *Ibid.*, 208.

Wesley felt that they had been spread generously in the writings. Another factor Wesley writes about is the concept of self-examination and finds in the treatise that Kempis writes not only about "gross sins," but also distinguished the difference between good thoughts and evil thoughts. Wesley found Kempis saying the reading of scripture and the taking and understanding of the Holy Communion was significant in a holy life. Wesley writes in his *Works* that Kempis' treatise instructs "us how to make Holy Communion an effectual means of Christian perfection."[193]

So, the natural question is, to what degree did Kempis influence Wesley? From what is found Wesley not only felt that this particular collection of writings should be studied but he would use it as the focus of his meditation. He felt it was something that should be brought into every fiber of the believers being. In Wesley's, *A Plain Account of Christian Perfection* there are a number of similarities to Thomas á Kempis' *The Imitation of Christ*. In the very beginning of Wesley's work, we find him mentioning Kempis and giving him a great deal of credit for a change in his own thoughts. He states that after reading Kempis' treatise he resolved to dedicate his whole life to God and wrote that every part of his life must be either sacrificed to

---

[193] *Ibid.*, 204, 205.

God or myself [Wesley], it is, in effect, to worship the devil.[194]

Reading Wesley, it becomes apparent that the two have many points in common with no actual differences, especially the concept of practical mysticism. The practical mysticism Wesley adopted combines the internal evidence and unshakable faith of speculative mysticism with the external life of constant service to both God and humanity. We find this in his writing,

. . . is a complete and finished work, comprehending all that relates to Christian perfection, all the principles of that internal workshop with which alone we worship God in spirit and truth.[195]

Wesley becomes even more specific where he says,

In order to attain this perfect love, there are several stages to be passed through: For it is necessary, not only to have the soul fully purged from all willful, habitual sin; but likewise that it be enlightened by the knowledge and practice of virtue, before it can be united to God.[196]

---

[194] John Wesley, *A Plain Account of Christian Perfection* ([1777) ed. Thomas Jackson (1872)] ed. George Lyons, (Nampa, ID: Northwest Nazarene College, 1996)), 1.
[195] Wesley, *Works, vol. XIV*, 204.
[196] *Ibid.*

At the summary of his text Wesley writes that those who want to follow God and seek the truth will find it if they dig deep into Kempis' work.

... yet it must be remembered that the great practical truths of religion, the mysteries of the inward kingdom of God cannot be fully discerned, but by those readers who have read the same thing in their own souls. . .[197]

Wesley agrees with Kempis' Christian mysticism and the various stages to achieve it and does not offer a reproof in any way. Kempis' expression of holiness and practical mysticism is endorsed by Wesley.

And herein it greatly resembles the Holy Scriptures, that under the plainest of words, there is divine hidden virtue, continually flowing into the soul of a pious and attentive reader, and by the blessing of God, transforming it into His image.[198]

Wesley in his synopsis of Kempis' treatise did not reference every chapter of the book, in some cases they were omitted because they would have been redundant to what he had written or because the topics were elemental to belief or doctrine. Overall, Wesley directly quoted or agreed with 100

---

[197] *Ibid.*, 207.
[198] *Ibid.*, 202.

out 119 chapters with little objection to any of the subjects not mentioned. If there were any differences in sentiments on certain subjects, they tended to be in point of view not belief. Wesley was writing as an Evangelical Anglican Methodist to his countrymen in defense of his doctrine. Kempis was writing as a Fifteenth Century cloistered monk who wrote to monks. A basic different point of view and audience but similarities in their doctrinal sentiments.

The idea of purity was common to both Wesley and Kempis. Wesley writes,

saw the 'simplicity of intention, and purity of affection,' on design in all we speak or do, and one desire ruling all our tempers, and indeed 'the wings of the soul,' without which she can never ascend to the mount of God.[199]

Kempis writes similarly,

A man is raised from earthly things with two wings; they are simplicity and purity. Simplicity should be your intention, purity your affection. Simplicity means following God, purity is knowing and loving him.[200]

---

[199] Wesley, *A Plain Account of Christian Perfection*, 2.
[200] Kempis. *The Imitation of Christ*, 24.

Purity was a concept found throughout both of their writings even though not always pronounced. Wesley made it a foundation of his writings,

. . . it is purity of intention, dedicating all the life to God. It is the giving God all our heart; it is one desire and design ruling all our tempers. It is the devoting, not a part, but all our soul, body, and substance to God.[201]

Kempis has essentially the same sentiment,

. . . seek nothing else but to please
God . . . if there is any joy in the world the man of a pure heart has it . . . a man who gives himself entirely to God is freed and taken from idleness and changed onto a new man . . .[202]

Kempis saw purity as a product of God and the heart because only a pure heart can be pleasing to God. There were also fruits/attributes that are displayed for it is life in Christ that makes one wise not the things of the earth. In fact, Kempis saw earthly wisdom hiding the truth and it was only after searching for God and striving for purity that wisdom is found. Kempis felt the wise must be

---

[201] Wesley, *A Plain Account of Christian Perfection*, 87.
[202] Kempis. *The Imitation of Christ*, 24.

82

taught by the spirit, paying no attention to private feeling, keeping their thoughts on God.[203]

Wesley agreed with the idea of purity as important and necessary. Perfect love would mean that the believer is acting the way God wants them to act, consciously watching their pattern of behavior and speech. The believer is giving their all to God, following where He leads,

. . . resolved to dedicate all [their] life to God, all [their] thoughts and words and actions; being thoroughly convinced, there is no medium; but that every part of [their] life must either be a sacrifice to God or [themselves], that is effect, to the devil.[204]

Wesley described it with a poem of Count Zinzendorf he translated in 1738 on his return trip from Savannah, Georgia,

O grant that nothing in my soul
May dwell, but thy pure love alone!
O may thy love possess me whole,
My joy, my treasure, and my crown!
Strange fires far from my heart remove;
My every act, word, thought, be love.[205]

---

[203] *Ibid.*, 2,3,24.
[204] Wesley, *A Plain Account of Christian Perfection*, 1.
[205] *Ibid.*, 4.

Purity of heart was not the only point of agreement for Wesley and Kempis, but they agreed that it came together naturally with meekness, gentleness and humility. Both men tried to achieve these characteristics feeling they were necessary to live a holy life.

When looking at the original Hebrew and Greek meekness means a mildness of disposition, a gentleness of spirit, the ability to become low, or depressed, or to be downcast.[206] Humble has a Biblical connotation of having a modest opinion of one's self, behaving in an unassuming manner devoid of all haughtiness. Gentleness means being mild, having moral goodness, integrity, benignity, and kindness.[207] These descriptive terms are used throughout both works.

Kempis saw the humble as those who served God more than those who sought the praise of humanity. He believed that the humble knew their true worth and ability, not wanting the praise of the world, realizing they may know many things and yet comprehend there is more to learn. They are unlike the educated, the educated who are anxious to seem knowledgeable and be thought wise but know little that will help the soul; "It is better to

---

[206] Ken Hamel, "Online Bible-Version 2.5.3," (Oakhurst, N.J.: Online Bible Software) Note: Hebrew – Meekness (עֲנָוָה); Greek – Meekness (Πραότητα), Humble (ταπεινός), Gentleness (ευγένεια).
[207] Wesley, *A Plain Account of Christian Perfection*, 6.

taste a little with humility and meekness, than to have treasures of cunning and vanity."[208]

Kempis saw the meek as those who walk in truth, simplicity of heart, and who think of their sins with displeasure and mourn over what they have done, never thinking any better of themselves because they have done something good or pleasant. In fact, he thought it was even better if one hid their devotion and tried not to rise too high, even taking upon the appearance of degrading one's self. "The meek man who suffers reproaches and wrongs is still at peace for he knows God is with him [them]. Know that you have not learned until you feel yourself lower than others."[209]

In *A Plain Account of Christian Perfection* Wesley treats humility and meekness the same as Kempis. He saw love as the purifier of the heart cleansing the believer from pride, and endowing the individual with the qualities of kindness, humbleness of mind, meekness, and long-suffering. He explains that to follow Christ one must be meek and gentle. Meekness means keeping the soul calm and temperate in all things.[210] Kempis had a similar understanding in keeping the soul in peace and quiet so that it can grow and learn the secrets of the scriptures.[211]

---

[208] Kempis. *The Imitation of Christ*, 2,39.

[209] *Ibid.*, 23, 36, 38.

[210] Wesley, *A Plain Account of Christian Perfection*, 7, 64.

[211] Kempis. *The Imitation of Christ*, 13.

Wesley's writings on Christian perfection shows how Wesley had assimilated Kempis's thinking. In Wesley's, *A Plain Account of Christian Perfection*, he addresses the most frequent questions about perfection:

Q-Suppose one had attained to this [perfect love], would you advise him to speak of it?

At first perhaps he would scarce be able to refrain, the fire would be so hot within him; his desire to declare the loving kindness of the Lord carrying him away like a torrent. But afterwards he might; and then it would beadvisable, not to speak of it to them that know not God; (it would most likely only provoke them to contradict and blaspheme;) nor to others, without some particular reason, without some good in view. And then he should have special care to avoid all appearance of boasting; to speak with the deepest humility and reverence giving all glory to God.[212]

Kempis similarly writes,

Son it is better and surer for you to hide your devotion and not try to raise yourself too high. Do not speak about
it. . .Do not discuss the works of God, but look to your sins. . .The man who can watch his words is the man who can keep his silence. . .Then shall you

---

[212] Wesley, *A Plain Account of Christian Perfection*, 36.

be rewarded for well-kept silence rather than long talking. Then shall Holy works be worth more than fair

woods. . . [213]

Looking at gentleness we find Wesley and Kempis agreeing again. Kempis sees the gentle person as one who follows the path God has laid out for them, suffering reproaches and wrongs, remaining at peace because they know God is with them.[214] Similarly Wesley writes that gentleness is a fruit of the spirit, a way we know we're abiding in Christ. He sees gentleness as without a touch of anger, even at the moment we are provoked.[215]

Reviewing Wesley's, *A Plain Account of Christian Perfection* there is abundant evidence of Wesley assimilating Kempis's *Imitation of Christ* having a major impact. Similar topics include the idea of resignation in God and to his will, of obedience, temptation, evil thoughts, purgation and the idea of being broken at the Cross of Christ. It is obvious from examining the *Imitation of Christ* that it significantly impacted Wesley's thinking and eventually his writings. One striking example is when we look at what Kempis' considers at the Cross of Christ.

---

[213] Kempis. *The Imitation of Christ*, 38, 37, 13,19.
[214] *Ibid.*, 23.
[215] Wesley, *A Plain Account of Christian Perfection*, 64.

The admonition, 'Deny thyself and take they cross and follow me' seems hard admonition to many people . . . Therefore, put yourself forward as a good and true servant and bravely carry the Cross of Christ. Be prepared to suffer adversities and discomforts in this wretched life, for he will be with you wherever you are, and you shall find Him wherever you seek . . . If you put yourself forward, as you should, to suffer and die, you shall find peace . . . How great an example for your neighbor? For all men admire patience, though few can suffer.[216]

Kempis is showing the value of waiting patiently on Christ as He works out His plan for a believer's life. Kempis instructs the believer what they may expect and how they should act in adversity and discomfort as an example to others. Wesley's treatise is a synthesis of Kempis' when Wesley writes about admonition and instruction,

Be patterns to all, of denying yourselves, and taking up your cross daily. Let them see that you make no account of any pleasure which does not bring you closer to God, nor regard any pain which does ; that you simply aim at pleasing Him, whether by doing or suffering; that the constant language of your heart, with regard to pleasure or pain, honor or

---

[216] Kempis. *The Imitation of Christ*, 30-33.

dishonor, riches or poverty, is, 'All's alike to me, so I, in my Lord may live and die!'[217]

After reviewing both works, *The Imitation of Christ* and *A Plain Account of Christian Perfection* it is apparent the level of assimilation of Kempis by Wesley. This should not be that surprising when one remembers Kempis had been introduced to Wesley by his mother.[218] In fact since the age of twenty-two the *Imitation of Christ* had been part of Wesley's life with his mother's recommendation of reading it daily. However, there are those who feel that Wesley eventually found Kempis's practices bring hardships to life and over all his fascination was short lived.[219]

This conclusion seems erroneous. From reading Wesley's synopsis of Kempis, he suggests that it should be read daily, and that it is important to prepare one's self praying using parts of the second and third books of the treaties for this prayer. Wesley even instructs the reader of the treatise not to read it just to stimulate the intellect but to read it to change the heart.[220]

There is also a great deal of scholarly evidence that Wesley was influenced and continued to be influenced by the writings of Kempis. Harold

---

[217] Wesley, *A Plain Account of Christian Perfection*, 64.
[218] Tuttle, *Mysticism in the Wesleyan Tradition*, 48.
[219] Clapper, *John Wesley on Religious Affections*, 128.
[220] Wesley, *Works, vol. XIV*, 208.

Linström, in his work *Wesley and Sanctification* writes,

A preliminary general idea of Wesley's doctrine of perfection is perhaps best obtained from the angle of its relation to practical mysticism of the type of Thomas á Kempis . . . In connection with this preliminary description of perfection reference might also be made to two epitomes by Wesley of his doctrine of perfection. The affinity to mysticism is particularly apparent in *A Plain Account of Christian Perfection*. Purity of intention, the imitation of Christ, and the wholehearted love of God . . . [221]

Linström supported the idea that Wesley was not only influenced by Kempis, but actually assimilated two of his paradigms.

There is little doubt that Wesley was deeply moved by Kempis as can be evidenced from how Wesley embraced his teachings on practical mysticism. When considering *A Plain Account of Christian Perfection* there are primary documents that define Wesley's personal doctrine and also his personal assimilation of Kempis' doctrine of practical mysticism. The question that begs to be answered is how far reaching was this mystical influence?

---

[221] Harold Linström, *Wesley and Sanctification*, 128,129.

Chapter 4 - The Influence of Mysticism on John Wesley's Theology.

When considering Wesley's doctrine on Christian perfection the question is how far reaching was mystical influence? William R. Cannon, Bishop of the United Methodist Church gives insight into the answer where he writes in the introduction to *Mysticism in the Wesleyan Tradition* that Rev. John Wesley was highly influenced by Christian mysticism and that it formed the essence of his doctrine of Christian perfection.[222]

In examining the various mystic authors that were familiar to John Wesley a number of different topics were explored including the stages that believers go through to reach mystical enlightenment. These stages of purification, illumination, and union with God for the Christian mystic culminates with knowing God directly and intimately with the experience possibly being void of intellectual knowledge or rationality. One experience mystics and Christian mystics undergo between the last two stages is a phenomenon known as the 'Dark Night of the Soul.' This is the time of

---

[222] Tuttle, *Mysticism in the Wesleyan Tradition*, 14.

soul searching and faith and the mystic must rely and trust only in God.

Wesley was also extremely interested and widely read in the Roman Catholic and protestant mystics responding to his contemporaries. These mystics contributed to his doctrine of Christian perfection in positive and negative ways. The Roman Catholic mystics from the Catholic Reformation contributed to his understanding of perfection, self-denial, and obedience. The Protestant mystics Wesley interacted with tended to be experientially oriented and would advocate times of outbursts, prophesying, and other demonstrative behaviors in their worship practices. During these times people would roll around on the floor, speak in prophetic languages and at time utter prophecies. Although the protestant mystics varied, they always had overtones of Christian piety.

Additionally, when looking at Wesley's Christian perfection in *A Plain Account of Christian Perfection* there are a number of similarities with Kempis' *Imitation of Christ*. There is ample evidence of Wesley assimilating Kempis especially in perfection, meekness, humility, and the ability to be gentle.

We have been discussing what appealed to Wesley about mysticism, however there are writings concerning Wesley rejecting mysticism. Francis McConnell in his book *John Wesley* writes the three foes of Christianity Wesley feared the most were

"Calvinism, Antinomianism, and Mysticism"[223] In a letter John Wesley wrote to brother Samuel in 1736, John Wesley said he was not aware the influence mysticism had on him. He said that mysticism was the "rock upon which he nearly made a shipwreck."[224] Wesley felt a passive "dark night" was not the way to obtain the perfect love he sought; he was too purposeful in his search for Christ.[225]

Wesley read Fénelon, Madame Guyon, Jacob Boehme, and William Law. These mystics are an example of the type Wesley had investigated; wrote to his brother Samuel about in 1736 and in some cases when he almost lost his faith, summarized their writings.[226] Wesley didn't embrace all mystics. One in particular he was doctrinally opposed to was Jacob Boehme who Wesley described as verbose, pretentious, and nothing but nonsense. Boehme "freely used Qabalist and alchemical symbolism to explain how an invisible, eternal, and infinite God could create and pervade a visible temporal world,"[227] Boehme felt God revealed Himself in an eternal cycle, the theognostic process.[228] Wesley rejected this type of mysticism, the pagan texture of

---

[223] Francis J. McConnell, *John Wesley*, (New York: Abington Press, 1939), 157.
[224] Wesley, *The Letters of John Wesley, vol I*, 207.
[225] Tuttle, *John Wesley: His Life and Theology*, 155.
[226] McConnell, *John Wesley*, 149.
[227] Cox, *Handbook of Christian Spirituality*, 192.
[228] *Ibid.*

mysticism that could be considered gnostic mysticism. He wanted nothing to do with a mystic way that left Christ out and skipped the form to get to the function. Wesley saw any mystic that didn't include Christ as occultic in style and Machiavellian in practice.

Wesley also rejected that part of mysticism found a great deal in the Middle Ages, solitary worship.[229] There is no doubt that when meditating or in praying may be performed alone, however there is no mandate or persuasion to perform severe hermitage or asceticism. In fact, in the 'New Testament' the opposite is found to be true with admonitions such as ". . . let us consider one another in order to stir up love and good not forsaking the assembly of ourselves together as is the manner of some . . ."[230] In Wesley's opinion Christianity was essentially a social religion turning; it into a solitary religion would cause its ruin.[231]

By a social religion Wesley was not thinking of it as merely manifesting itself into society as in public but the togetherness of being together, worshipping together, and helping each other out. Wesley saw much more in being a Christian. When he looked at mysticism, he saw a personal quest but Christianity he conceived of it as a field of practice

---

[229] W.T. Purkiser, *Exploring Our Christian Faith*, (Kansas City, MO: Beacon Hill Press, 1978), 386. [Wesley "Sermon on the Mount" Discourse IV]
[230] Hebrews 10: 24, 25 (NKJV)
[231] Purkiser, *Exploring Our Christian Faith*, 386.

and experience in use as a corrective measure. Wesley saw Christianity as a reinforcement of personal experience hence the Methodist practice of class meetings. Christians were never meant to live in solitude, nor to act too exclusively on their own interpretation of scripture, coming together to worship and share.

There is evidence that could be used to show that Wesley rejected mysticism. He certainly didn't care for solitary mysticism that by-passed the worship of Christ. There are those who would use this evidence to say that Wesley's criticism is exaggerated and the term mystic so blurred that it could be incorporated into anything. Attempting to jump over these difficulties regardless of plausibility and paint Wesley with a mystic brush won't work.[232] At least this is a reasonable conclusion if one neglects the different aspects of mysticism.

Although there is a great deal of evidence to support that Wesley rejected mysticism and by some standards he did, however there was a great deal that was used. The aspect of mysticism Wesley did reject was Speculative Mysticism, that part that is merely an internal evidence and internal faith with no practical application or outward expression. Wesley embraced practical mysticism that includes

---

[232] W.E. Sangster, *The Path to Perfection: An Examination and Restatement of John Wesley's Doctrine of Christian Perfection*, (New York: Abington-Cokesbury Press, 1943) 147.

the internal saving faith and internal evidence but with external service to God and humanity.

In our examination of Wesley and his writings it is apparent that he was well read in the doctrine and theology of the mystics. Some of the mystic writings were far from where Wesley was theologically whereas others were accepted by him in whole or in part. The mystics Wesley read didn't come from any denomination or theological tradition and he studies both Protestant and Roman Catholic traditions. He devoured groups like the French prophets, the Moravians, German mystics, and especially Thomas á Kempis and 'Methodist mystic' John Fletcher. Wesley's investigation at this time was the search for the standards and needs of Christian living. His studies led him to synthesize the "perfectionism of the pietist, the moralism of the Puritans, and the devotionalism of the mystics in a pragmatic approach that he felt could operate within the doctrine of the Church of England."[233] This synthesis was important because from it came the concepts and designs of Christian mysticism that were well known by Wesley and flavored his doctrine. At times it's been called Christian perfection, but has also been identified with sanctification, holiness, and perfect love.[234]

The word perfection, as with mystic and mysticism, has its own history and special

---

[233] Heitzenrater, *Wesley and the people Called Methodist*, 31.
[234] Sangster, *The Path to Perfection*, 144.

understanding with the same defect as the term mysticism, it's ambiguous. This ambiguity "it shares the [with] same word *teleios* (τέλειος) both are employed now in a relative, now in an absolute sense."[235] When the concept of perfection is viewed in a doctrinal sense in various sects the meaning changes. Either perfection means nothing at all or expresses something that can never be attained. Wesley trying to define perfection at times adds a twist and to some even more vagueness. Wesley writing in *The Letters of John Wesley*, volume III,

. . . loving God with all our heart and serving Him with all our strength. Nor did I ever say or mean any more of perfection than thus loving and serving God.[236]

Wesley writes again in volume VII,

Entire Sanctification, or Christian Perfection, is neither more or less pure love – love expelling sin and governing both the heart and life of a child of God.[237]

Christian perfection was an important concept for Wesley's entire life; a concept that was frequently mentioned in his journals, letters, and

---

[235] *Ibid.*
[236] Wesley, *The Letters of John Wesley, vol III*, 168.
[237] Wesley, *The Letters of John Wesley, vol VII*, 120

sermons. From the first time he was exposed to practical mysticism in 1723, Wesley never abandoned his position on Christian Perfection.[238] The practical mysticism that infected him the most was that of Thomas á Kempis, where Wesley saw true religion was seated in the heart, and that the law of God extended to thoughts as well as actions and words.[239] Wesley had the same belief on practical mysticism and Christian perfection his entire life as shown by writings just prior to his death. A year before his death Wesley writes,

"This doctrine [practical mysticism/Christian perfection] is the grand deposition which God has lodged with the people of the Methodist; and for the sake of propagating this chiefly He appeared to have raised us up."[240] Wesley never contemplated Christian perfection or Methodism being outside the Anglican church, He saw perfection as a divinely inspired quest by all Christians. Wesley is found penning an answer to a tract entitled *Imposture Detected* by Rowland Hill where he writes,

The perfection I hold is so far from being contrary to the doctrine of the church, that is exactly the same which every clergyman prays for every Sunday" 'Cleanse the thoughts of our hearts by the

---

[238] Linström, *Wesley and Sanctification*, 126.
[239] Clapper, *John Wesley on Religious Affections*, 128.
[240] Wesley, *The Letters of John Wesley, vol VIII*, 238.

inspiration of the Holy Spirit, that we may perfectly love Thee, and worthily worship thy Holy name.'[241]

Wesley's doctrine of perfection can be traced to the practical mysticism of Kempis and the Anglican Churchmen Jeremy Taylor and William Law. Taylor and Law favored the Arminian direction of the church. Wesley found in the *Imitation of Christ* two paradigms he uses in *A Plain Account of Christian Perfection* written in 1766.[242] These paradigms were a purity of intentions and a wholehearted love of God and our neighbors.

In one view, it is purity of intention, dedicating all the life to God. It is the giving God all our heart; it is one desire and design ruling all tempers. It is devoting, not a part, but all our soul, body, and substance to God. In another view, it is all the mind, which was in Christ, enabling us to walk as Christ walked. It is the circumcision of the heart from all filthiness, all inward as well as outward pollution. It is a renewal of the heart in the whole image of God, in full likeness of Him that created it. In yet another, it is the loving God with all our heart, and our neighbor as ourselves.[243]

---

[241] Wesley, *Works, vol. X*, 450.
[242] Linström, *Wesley and Sanctification*, 128, 131.
[243] Wesley, *A Plain Account of Christian Perfection*, 87.

Factors for determining perfection are purity of intention, the imitation of Christ, and whole-hearted love of God and our neighbors. Wesley was in full agreement with practical mysticism; both inward and outward holiness is necessary. The differences between what Wesley believed and what was taught by Kempis was insignificant even after Wesley's Aldersgate experience in 1738. It is true that the experience did influenced his doctrine and life. Before 1738, Wesley felt that perfection was a gradual development towards inward and outward holiness. An inherent personal holiness, a purity and piety of the heart and the mind.[244] For Wesley saw the Christian life as serious effort at self-denial and taking up the cross daily.[245] After his experience at Aldersgate St. Wesley no longer saw perfection as only attainable at death. He still had the very practical mystic understanding of holiness being a state of repentance and of sincerity of heart and diligent behavior.[246] The difference was that he no longer felt that state of imperfection and repentance till death. After 1738, Wesley felt that perfection was something that could be realized in the believer's lifetime.[247] Wesley now saw it as a gift of God and a work of the Holy Spirit. This personal revelation changed his view of grace, gave a new look at justification and impacted his doctrine of

---

[244] Linström, *Wesley and Sanctification*, 131, 132.
[245] Wesley, *A Plain Account of Christian Perfection*, 37.
[246] Wesley, *The Letters of John Wesley, vol I*, 48.
[247] Wesley, *The Letters of John Wesley, vol IV*, 11, 192.

perfection. Wesley believed that usually the Christian did not obtain perfection until death or shortly before death.[248] Wesley's doctrine changed and included the possibility that perfection could come not only at death or shortly before, but any time before death and come instantly. Christian perfection, also known as entire sanctification, is seen as coming through sanctifying faith, by intervention of God himself, this is what makes it possible to be an instant work.[249]

Wesley did believe in a gradual work of sanctification; he merely taught that entire sanctification, or Christian perfection, was an additional stage in our Christian walk after salvation. Wesley saw sanctification as a work that could be gradual or instantaneous in the salvation process. In fact, Wesley sees the whole process in stages; first saved by instantaneous salvation, after which there follows a gradual sanctification, and then following another instantaneous event called entire sanctification (Christian perfection), with a gradual increase of holiness. Wesley felt that the gradual work of sanctification was a prerequisite for the instantaneous work of sanctification and that this meant obedience to the ordinances and commandments of God.[250]

---

[248] Wesley, *Works, vol. VIII*, 294, 341.
[249] Wesley, *A Plain Account of Christian Perfection*, 13.
[250] *Ibid.*, 13, 41, 134.

Although Wesley did not adopt all of mysticism, it is readily seen that many mystical attributes were used especially that which was part of the practical mystics. This can be seen in Wesley's affinity for mystical piety and devotion; a theme that stayed with him his entire life.

Another aspect of Wesley's theology is the value he placed on religious experience. Mysticism in general has the distinctive of the ultimate experience of uniting with God. Unity with God speaks not only regarding a special illuminated union, but also experiencing God in our lives. God's presence will spiritually change us but can also give us joyous expressions and an extinction of the past which spiritually hamper us. Kempis in his treatise writes of this,

I shall hear what Christ says to me. Happy is the soul that hears Christ speaking in him and takes from his mouth the word of consolation. Blessed are those that receive the words of God and pay no attention to the words of the world.
Happy is he whom truth herself teaches, not by colorful speech or empty words, but by her own essence . . . The more a man is one with God the more he will understand, for his light of understanding comes from above.
My Lord God . . . what you come into my heart all shall exalt [You] . . . The pure love of Christ helps me to do great things and encourages me to wish

perfection . . . The lover of God dances and sings and is glad.

Turn with all your heart to God and give up this wretched world . . . Learn to renounce all outward things and give yourself to the matters of your soul and you shall feel the Kingdom of God.[251]

When reviewing mysticism, the experience can play a part in the spiritual development of the believer. Kempis certainly talked about and implied experiences as a result of practical holiness. St. John of the Cross, and St. Teresa both spoke of mysticism and the effects of mystical experience on the believer. Experience had been part of Wesley's doctrine and basic theological outlook; the problem was what Wesley meant by experience. The majority of the time he uses it as a catch phrase or can be seen as a term that "encompasses many kinds of different, individual experiences."[252] Wesley saw experience in terms of the Fruit of the Spirit, as in feeling loved, having joy, and being at peace, more in line with the experiences of the mystics. However, Wesley did feel that experiences could take many forms, positive or negative, at the beginnings of a new life or at the death throes of an old one.

Wesley proposed at one time that ecstasies and convulsion were a necessary part of the conversion

[251] Kempis. *The Imitation of Christ*, 34, 2, 3, 37, 22.
[252] Clapper, *John Wesley on Religious Affections*, 2.

experience.[253] In fact, many in Wesley's audiences would often be subject to convulsions, some feeling strong pain, others breaking down into tears and cries.[254] Then there were others that exhibited extremely strange behavior with some being afflicted by laughter. One woman laughed until almost strangled, and then began cursing.[255] Wesley wrote that for two days those inflicted laughed continually until the group that had gathered together prayed over them until they were delivered.[256] John Cennick, the first layman of the movement to preach, was placed in charge, for a time, of the Kingswood School which was started by Wesley in 1748. While preaching at the school he reported many experiencing the same or similar type of phenomena that Wesley observed. During the preaching of his sermon there were those who would be tormented and through the power of prayer were delivered. When these types of experiences occurred, there was almost always a deliverance. Wesley once saw these types of experiences as a necessary feature of salvation with the experiences continuing to occur during Wesley's preaching to those destroyed by sin and the devil. After 1740 however the outcries and

[253] Wesley, *The Journal of the Rev. John Wesley, vol. II*, 246.
[254] Schwartz, *The French Prophets*, 205.
[255] Garret, *Spirit Possession and Popular Religion*, 87.
[256] Wesley, *The Journal of the Rev. John Wesley, vol. II*, 342.

convulsions during his preaching happened considerably less.[257]

Another experience that Wesley commented on is being entirely sanctified by faith. The work came by faith yet within the context of sanctification and seeking after the will of God. By Wesley's definition those who were entirely sanctified no longer knowingly committed sin and were declared perfect. Wesley explained,

By justification we are saved from the quilt of sin and restored to the favor of God; by sanctification we are saved from the power and root of sin and restored to the image of God. All experience, as well as Scripture, show this salvation to be both instantaneous and gradual. It begins in the moment . . . till in another instant, the heart is cleansed from all sin, and filled with pure love of God and man.[258]

This type of experience demonstrates a semi-mystical discernment of how our spirit grows over time. The influence that practical mysticism had on the doctrine of gradual sanctification and how it worked with entire sanctification was significant. Entire sanctification has its base in the holy life of the believer with the origin of this holy life in a mystical religious experience.[259] We find this in the

---

[257] Garret, *Spirit Possession and Popular Religion*, 86-88.
[258] Wesley, *Works, vol. VI*, 294, 509.
[259] Metz, *Studies in Biblical Holiness*, 14.

writings of Thomas Cook and his description of holiness,

. . . an experience distinct from justification – a sort of supplemental conversion, in which there is eliminated from the soul all sinful elements which do not belong to it, everything from antagonistic to the elements of holiness implanted in regeneration. It includes the full cleansing of the soul from inbred sin, so that it becomes pure or free from sinful tendency.[260]

Holiness is viewed as an experience of the soul not a contrived legalistic process of the physical body. Wesley blended his non-legalistic doctrine and assimilated practical mysticism into doctrine and theology.

Wesley's Aldersgate-heart-strangely-warmed experience was prefaced with his missionary experience in North America. Wesley arrived back from the Georgia colony early in 1738. He had a hard time in the colonies, the Native Americans didn't receive him well and in a strange way he felt the mystics had left him. Wesley returned to England dejected and learned little from his trial by fire, feeling no closer to faith, peace, or assurance.[261]

---

[260] Thomas Cook, *New Testament Holiness*, (London: Epworth Press, 1902), 7,8.
[261] Tuttle, *Mysticism in the Wesleyan Tradition*, 142.

In 1738, "Francis Wynantz, a German born merchant who was a sometime follower of the French Prophet Hannah Wharton,"[262] opened his house for a meeting between John Wesley and Peter Böhler. Wesley became convinced that conversion was instantaneous and, in a sense, miraculous. Charles Wesley was upset with his brother John and his change in doctrine. The opposition changed "when he [Charles]himself underwent conversion on May 21, 1738."[253] Then on May 24, 1738 Wesley attended a meeting at Aldersgate St. and while someone was reading Luther's preface to the *Book of Romans* Wesley's heart was strangely warmed, The meeting had been arranged by Böhler and James Hutton with Wesley originally being reluctant to go.[264] This experience changed Wesley and from that time forward he truly did trust Christ for his salvation. Kempis had revealed to Wesley that holiness must be a person's final purpose, however he also felt that giving his life to God was nothing unless he gave his heart to God too.[265]

Although in a scientific sense the experience at Aldersgate is subjective in nature yet it is the turning point in Wesley's life. Wesley himself said that he had gone from the faith and state of a servant

---

[262] Garret, *Spirit Possession and Popular Religion*, 77.
[263] *Ibid.*
[264] *Ibid.*
[265] Green, *John Wesley*, 59.

107

to that of an adopted son of God.[266] An experience such as this, similar to the process of sanctification (differing from entire sanctification), would be the inauguration into the mystical process.[267] Tuttle writing in *Mysticism in the Wesleyan Tradition* saw Aldersgate as the end of a nineteen-month wrestling match with the doctrine of the mystics. Although Wesley and the mystics maintained a common end, particularly the doctrine of perfection, Tuttle asserts Wesley's doctrine was significantly different. He postulates that Wesley replaced the mystic's dark night of the soul with the evangelical doctrine of justification by faith.[268]

Aldersgate was the moment that the doctrine of justification was sealed within Wesley's distinctives. His writings after Aldersgate didn't seem to decisively nullify the concept of the dark night of the soul. Later that night after the experience at the meeting Wesley wrote,

After I returned home, I was much buffeted with temptations; but cried out and they fled away. They returned again and again. I often lifted up my eyes, and 'He sent me help from his holy place.'[269]

---

[266] David A. Cubie, *Placing Aldersgate in John Wesley's Order of Salvation*, (Wesley Theological Society: Altavista.com [search -Aldersgate]. 1988)

[267] M. James Sawyer, PhD, *Wesleyan & Keswick Models of Sanctification*, (San Jose, CA: Western Seminary, 1997), 4.

[268] Tuttle, *Mysticism in the Wesleyan Tradition*, 18.

[269] Wesley, *Works, vol. I*, 103.

In November 1739, Wesley, writing in his journal, maintains that those who believe should be aware of two opposite extremes. Either thinking that while in light and joy the work has ended when it's just begun or that when we are in heaviness that the work hasn't begun, because it hasn't ended.

Aldersgate seems to have served as a step in Wesley's development and a further assimilation of the mystic way, but not the end. Throughout his life he knew justification was by faith, however, he looked upon sanctification as his assurance of faith. In a way it led to Wesley going through the mystical process of repeated periods of illumination, darkness and then union. Wesley writes numerous times of instances of a dark period before a union.

On October 14, 1738 he wrote, "I cannot find myself thy love God, or of Christ. Hence my deadness and wanderings in public prayer . . . Again: I find I have not that joy in the Holy Ghost"

On January 4, 1739 he wrote, "My friends affirm I am mad, because I said I was not a Christian a year ago. I affirm I am mad because I said I was not a Christian a year ago. I affirm I am not a Christian now. Indeed, what I might have been I know not . . . Though I have constantly used all means of grace for twenty years, I am not a Christian."

On June 27, 1766 he wrote to Charles Wesley, ". . . and yet (this is the mystery) I do not love God. I never did. Therefore, I never believed in the

Christian sense of the word. Therefore, I am only an honest heathen."[270]

The experience of Aldersgate did not lead to uninterrupted joy, there are found entries that point to gloom, doubt, and questioning periodically.[271]

When placing Aldersgate in its proper perspective and looking at it in the context of the modern holiness movement, it is found to be similar to the Pentecost experience.[272] Wesley is one who believes in being empowered for service through a mystical interaction with God, through Christ. Here Wesley has his Pentecost with the Holy Spirit, leaving his heart strangely warmed, ready for service and a clearer understanding of God. Aldersgate was a trigger experience to later union. Aldersgate didn't replace the dark night of the soul but was the culmination of it and served as the launch point for Wesley's union with God.

There is actually a great deal of agreement on Wesley and his mysticism between scholars. Respected scholars such as Tuttle, Green, McConnell, Canon, Sawyer, Cubie, Sangster, Heizenrater, and even Clapper generally agree there was some assimilation of mysticism by Wesley into his doctrine of Christian perfection and theology.

---

[270] Sawyer, PhD, *Wesleyan & Keswick Models of Sanctification*, 10.
[271] McConnell, *John Wesley*, 64.
[272] Cubie, *Placing Aldersgate in John Wesley's Order of Salvation*, 47.

110

There are those who see the whole situation of Wesley and mysticism as a personal fondness and respect for the pious life they lived. There are others, as Tuttle, that Wesley actually agreed and, in a way, practicing the stages of the mystic way. Some agree that there is a reasonable amount of acceptance that Wesley agreed with the aspects of purgation and illumination of the mystic way.[273] Purgation has always been part of the Methodist tradition. Wesley writes about it in *A Plain Account of Christian Perfection*,

Restore, and make me meet for heaven. Unless thou purge my every stain, Thy suffering and my faith is vain . . . Thy own peculiar servant claim. For thy own truth and mercy's sake, Hallow in me thy glorious name; me for thine own this moment take; And change and thoroughly purity; Thine only may I live and die . . . Purge me from every sinful blot: My idols cast aside: Cleanse me from every evil thought,. From all the filth of self and pride.[274]

Illumination is also a part of Wesley's belief and begins in the concentration of all upon God. "It differs from purgative life, not in discarding good works, but having come to perform them no longer as virtues . .[but] . . . willing and almost

---

[273] Tuttle, *Mysticism in the Wesleyan Tradition*, 126,127.
[274] Wesley, *A Plain Account of Christian Perfection*, 21,22.

spontaneously."[275]   Wesley writing about illumination or receiving light,

God usually gives a considerable time for men to receive light, to grow in grace, to do and suffer his will . . . On every occasion of uneasiness, we should retire to prayer, that we may give place to grace and light of God and then form our resolutions, without being in any pain about what success they may have.[276]

The last stage, union with God, is not just a part of Wesley's doctrine but Biblical as well. Throughout the Bible we are exhorted to invite God into our heart, taking off the old man and putting on the new, being filled with the Holy Spirt, a Pentecost type mysticism. There seems to be little problem with the general stages of mysticism, the problem seems to be the stage called dark night of the soul.

The dark night of the soul is seen by Christian mystics as a period of emptiness and stagnation. Dark because no indisputable vision occurs and at times seems nothing can be discerned, nothing "seen, smelled or heard as in the distinct visions of senses or imagination."[277] Tuttle and others see the dark night being replaced by the understanding of

---

[275] Inge, *Christian Mysticism*, 12.
[276] Wesley, *A Plain Account of Christian Perfection*, 64, 80.
[277] Dupré, *The Deeper Life: An Introduction to Christian Mysticism*, 82.

justification and the Aldersgate experience. No doubt Aldersgate made an impact on Wesley and his theology but did not replace the dark night of the soul, but rather signaled its end.

Although there is a wide variety of opinions concerning mysticism, it certainly played an important part in the life of Wesley and impacted his theology in a very real sense. From investigating John Wesley's life, his experiences and writings, we see that mysticism shaped his personal life and had a major impact on his outlook on sanctification and holiness. There is ample evidence that practical mysticism doctrinally and theologically formed the background and basis of not only Wesley's work, *A Plain Account of Christian Perfection*, but also the special aspects of his doctrine, which included holiness, sanctification, and in its fullest form entire sanctification.

Literature Review

There is not a large body of works concerning John Wesley and mysticism that is readily accessible, however, there are some significant contributions in the form of monographs and other sources concerning the subject.

Significant research into the influence of mysticism on Wesleyan theology is included in two significant works: *Mysticism in the Wesleyan Tradition* and *John Wesley: His Life and Theology* both written by Dr. Robert G. Tuttle. Both of these works touch on Wesley's theology and his connection with mysticism and various mystics.

Tuttle's book, *Mysticism in the Wesleyan Tradition* examines in-depth Wesley's understanding of mysticism and some of its early influences on him. Tuttle discusses Wesley's early experiments in mysticism and in Tuttle's view his reluctant rejection. Tuttle's other work, *John Wesley: His Life and Theology,* seems to be more of a chronological history of Wesley's life, however it does fill in a number of significant aspects of his time in Germany and his contacts with Peter Böhler.

Other sources consulted included *Studies in Biblical Holiness* by Donald Metz. This source takes an in-depth look at Biblical holiness and sanctification. Metz deals with a number of different aspects of holiness and gives each a full treatment. Sections of his work include topics such as mystical interpretation of holiness, sin and its variance with holiness, the idea of holiness as a spiritual dynamic, and the work of the Holy Spirit in holiness.

The Path to Perfection by Dr. W. E. Sangster looks into the life and theology of Wesley. Although the author treats Wesley's mysticism negatively that does not diminish his grasp on Wesley's life. His book is divided into segments each treating different aspects of Wesley's life and understandings. Sangster looks at Wesley through his approach to the Bible and believes Wesley was in full harmony with the New Testament and its writers.

Gregory S. Clapper's book *John Wesley on Religious Affections: His views on Experience and Emotion and their Role in Christian Life and Theology* is a revision of Clapper's PhD dissertation. It centers on "Wesley's theological reflection concerning the 'inner life'"[278] The source investigates closely aspects of his theology not treated in other sources.

There are a number of other works that are important to understanding Wesley, his theology, and mysticism. One of these works is *Christian Mysticism* by W. R. Inge. Although written in 1899

---

[278] Gregory S. Clapper, book *John Wesley on Religious Affections: His views on Experience and Emotion and their Role in Christian Life and Theology* (Metuchen, NJ: The Scarecrow Press, 1989) 9.

it has a series of eight lectures covering different aspects of Christian mysticism especially the historical background of speculative and practical mysticism. Another source is by Harold Linström entitled *Wesley and Sanctification*. One of the chapters *Christian Perfection* deals with the importance and significance of the doctrine of Christian Perfection and its interrelationship with mysticism.

The *Handbook of Christian Spirituality* by Michael Cox is by the author's own admission merely a starting point for a "deeper acquaintance with Christian mystical tradition."[279] The book deals first with the foundations of mysticism and includes the nature of mysticism and mysticism in the Bible. Cox then proceeds with an historical overview with the book being divided into two sections, *Early Church Fathers to the Spanish Carmelites* and *Mysticism Since 1600*.

One author who is indispensable to the topic of Mysticism is Evelyn Underhill. Her work *Mystics of the Church* is basically an historical examination of Christian mystics from Biblical times through the early church to those found in various national religious mystic movements and ends with a chapter on mode mystics. One of Underhill's most acclaimed books is *Mysticism* first published in 1911and is seen as a benchmark on the subject. The

---

[279] Michael Cox, *Handbook of Christian Spirituality* (San Francisco: Harper and Row Publishers, 1985) 13.

book itself is divided into two parts. One section she calls *Mystical Fact* where she deals with the mysticism with such aspects as psychology, theology, symbolism, and even magic. The other section called the *Mystic Way* explores the interaction of the individual person and mysticism. Subsections in her book investigate awakening, purification, illumination of the self, dark night of the soul, and the unitive life. The work although written early in the 20th century demonstrates remarkable grasp of the topic even for the reader of today.

Two other works of Underhill should be included here. *The Life of the Spirit of Today*, written in 1922 was an "attempt to harmonize classic expressions of the spiritual life with the insights of modern psychology."[280] The other work of hers is *The Spiritual Life* which is a transcript of four radio broadcasts, from 1937. They deal with different aspects of the spiritual life ranging from what the spiritual life is to our common union with God to our cooperation with God.

A number of primary sources were used in the creation of this book. Writings of John Wesley were used and included *Devotion and Prayers of John Wesley*, *The Journal of John Wesley*, Wesley's *Explanatory Notes Upon the New testament* and the complete *Works of John Wesley* were referenced.

---

[280] Evelyn Underhill, *The Life of the Spirit and the Life of Today* (San Francisco: Harper and Row Publishers, 1986) xii.

Other primary sources used but not authored by Wesley include *The Way of Perfection* by Teresa of Avila, the *Ascent of Mount Carmel* by St. John of the Cross and *The Silent Life* by Thomas Merton.

Teresa of Avila's (Teresa of Ávila) work depicts her desire to teach a deep and lasting love of prayer and prayer filled life. She writes about fraternal love, a detachment from material things and true humility. Avila councils the reader on the fruit of lofty speculation with mature practical experience developing these ideas into subjects of prayer and contemplation.[281]

St. John of the Cross and his *Ascent of Mount Carmel* is known as a guide to spiritual life. Its purpose was to inform Christians who wish to grow a deeper relationship with God and how it was done. He examines all the categories of the spiritual experience, from the authentic to the spurious.[282] The work is known as a treatise on Quietistic Mysticism.[283]

Thomas Merton is a 20th century monk who was searching for the 'truth.' Merton's work describes various branches of mystic family and offers an instructional understanding of this branch

---

[281] St. Teresa of Avila, *The Way of Perfection* (1565), ed. E. Allison Peers (Garden City, New York: Image Books, 1964) back cover.

[282] St. John of the Cross, *Ascent of Mount Carmel* (1580), ed. E. Allison Peers (Garden City, New York: Image Books, 1958) back/editors' comments.

[283] W. R. Inge, *Christian Mysticism* (London: Methuen, 1899) 224.

of the church.[284] The author describes the monastic peace, the cenobitic life, and finally the hermit life and within this context touches on a number of mystic characteristics and stages.

Two other primary sources that are explored thoroughly are *A Plain Account of Christian Perfection* by John Wesley and *The Imitation of Christ* by Thomas á Kempis. Wesley's work gives a history as to how he embraced Christian Perfection. The account covers the period between 1725 to 1777 with a number of revisions during this time, however after 1777 there were no major changes. The edition used as a source for this book is the 1872 publication edited by Thomas Jackson with this being the final collection of thoughts by Wesley since there were no later editions than 1777.

Thomas á Kempis was an Augustine monk that wrote the treatise *The Imitation of Christ* in 1441. Kempis' work was rendered into English by Giles Barton and exemplifies Western Mysticism. The author relates what he found to be Christian Perfection and the principles of internal worship. Mikhail Strabo, writing the introduction of the 1942 edition states that Kempis' writing "exhorts the reader to leave all behind and follow Christ in humility and faith."[285]

---

[284] Thomas Merton, *The Silent Life*, (New York: Dell Publishing Co., Inc., 1956) back/editor's comments.
[285] Thomas á Kempis, *The Imitation of Christ,* (1450) ed. Giles Barton (New York: Guidance House, 1942) vi.

Bibliography

Bainton, Roland H., *Here I Stand: A Life of Martin Luther*, Nashville: Abington Press, 1978

Caimana, Sister Rose Aquin, *Mysticism in Gabriela Mistral*, Bew York: Pageant Press International Corp., 1969

Clapper, Gregory S., *John Wesley on Religious Affections: His Views on Experience and Emotion and their Role in Christian Life and Theology*, Metuchen, New Jersey: The Scarecrow Press, Inc., 1989

Cox, Michael, *Handbook of Christian Spirituality*, San Francisco: Harper & Row Publishers, 1983

Cubie, David A., *Placing Aldersgate in John Wesley's Order of Salvation*, (Wesley Theological Society: Altavista.com [search -Aldersgate]. 1988

Dupré, Louis, *The Deeper Life: An Introduction to Christian Mysticism*, New York: Crossroad Publishing, 1981

Eastlack, Anita, Kerry D. Kind, Jerry Lumston, Matthew Pickering, Mark A. Rennaker, Johanna Rugh, Ronald C. McClung, co-chair, and Janelle Vernon, chair, *The Discipline of the Wesleyan Church 2016*, Indianapolis, Indiana: Wesleyan Publishing House, 2016

Fra. Apfelman, *The Dark Night of the Soul*, In Inner Sanctum Networks [electronic bulletin board] (March 1, 1997)

Garret, Clarke, *Spirit Possession and Popular Religion: From the Camisards to the Shakers*, Baltimore: The John Hopkins University Press, 1987

Green, V.H.H., *John Wesley*, London: Thomas Nelson and Sons, Ltd., 1964

Hamel, Ken, "Online Bible-Version 2.5.3," Oakhurst, N.J.: Online Bible Software

Hexman, Irving, *Concise Dictionary of Religion*, Downers Grove, Illinois: Intervarsity Press, 1993

Holidays, Festivals, and Celebrations of the World Dictionary, Fourth Edition. S.v. "Aldersgate Experience." Retrieved June 22, 2020 from https://encyclopedia2.thefreedictionary.com/Aldersgate+Experience

Inge, W.R., *Christian Mysticism*, London: Methuse, 1899

James, William, *Varieties of religious Experience*, New York: Longmans, Green, 1919

Kempis, Thomas á, *The Imitation of Christ* (1450) ed. Giles Barton, New York: Guidance House, 1942

Knox, Ronald, *Enthusiasm*, Oxford: Clarendon Publ., 1950

Linström, Harold, *Wesley and Sanctification*, New York: Abington Press, 1946

M'clintock, D.D., Rev, John, and James Strong, S.T.D., *Cyclopædia of Biblical, Theological, and Ecclesiastical Literature*, New York: Harper and Brothers Publishers, 1872

McConnell, Francis J., *John Wesley*, New York: Abingdon Press, 1939

Merton, Thomas, *The Silent Life*, New York: Dell Publishing Co., Inc., 1956

Metz, Donald S., *Studies in Biblical Holiness*, Kansas City, Missouri: Beacon Hill Press, 1971

Newman, Albert Henry, *A Manual of Church History*, Chicago: The American Baptist Publication Society, 1947

Purkiser, W.T., *Exploring Our Christian Faith*, Kansas City, MO: Beacon Hill Press, 1978

Reid, Daniel, ed. *Dictionary of Christianity in America*, Dowers Grove, Illinois: Intervarsity Press, 1990

St. John of the Cross, *Ascent of Mount Carmel* (1580), ed. E. Alison Peers, Garden City, New York: Image Books, 1958

St. Teresa of Avila, *The Way of Perfection* (1565) ed. E. Alison Peers, Garden City, New York: Image Books, 1964

Sangster, W.E., *The Path to Perfection: An Examination and Restatement of John Wesley's Doctrine of Christian Perfection*, New York: Abington-Cokesbury Press, 1943

Sawyer, PhD, M., *Wesleyan & Keswick Models of Sanctification*, San Jose, CA: Western Seminary, 1997

Schwartz, Hillel, *The French Prophets: The History of a Millenarian Group in Eighteenth-Century England*, Berkley: University of California Press, 1948

Smith, Barbara, *The Westminster Concise Bible Dictionary*, Philadelphia: Westminster Press, 1975

Tuttle, Jr., Robert G, Mysticism in the Wesleyan Tradition, Grand Rapids Michigan: Francis Asbury Press, 1989

Underhill, Evelyn, *Man and Supernatural*, New York: E. P. Dutton & Co., Inc., 1931

Mysticism: A Study in the Nature and Development of a Man's Spiritual Consciousness, New York: E.P. Dutton & Co., Inc., 1961

The Mystics of the Church, New York: Schocken Books, 1964

Wallenchinsky, David and Irving Wallace, *The People's Almanac*, Garden City, New York: Doubleday and Co., Inc. 1975

Wesley, John, *A Plain Account of Christian Perfection* [(1777) ed. Thomas Jackson (1872)] ed. George Lyons, Nampa, ID: Northwest Nazarene College, 1996

Ecclesiastical History, London: printed by J. Paramore, 1781

The Journal of the Rev. John Wesley, (1735-1791) ed. Nhehemiah Curnock, London: Epworth, 1909

Works, Bristol: printed by William Pine, 1771